JOHN HOWARD'S
Inside Guide to
ADVANCED PROPERTY DEVELOPING & INVESTING

John Howard

Matador
9 Priory Business Park,
Wistow Road, Kibworth Beauchamp,
Leicestershire LE8 0RX
Tel: 0116 279 2299
Email: books@troubador.co.uk
Web: www.troubador.co.uk/matador
Twitter: @matadorbooks

ISBN 978 1838592 998

British Library Cataloguing in Publication Data.
A catalogue record for this book is available from the British Library.

Printed and bound in Great Britain by 4edge Limited

Matador is an imprint of Troubador Publishing Ltd

ABOUT THE AUTHOR

John Howard is one of the most experienced property developers in the UK today. He secured his first property deal on his 18th birthday and has gone on to buy and sell 3,500 houses and flats across the UK, in a career that spans 35 years so far.

This gives John a unique insight into the business of property development, coupled with the fact that he was a Director and Shareholder for nine years of Auction House UK – the number one property auction business in the country, growing the franchise from seven to 42 auction houses. Along with his partners, John also owns the Norfolk franchise for the highly respected Fine & Country estate agency brand.

Although his focus is now on developing large schemes – such as the £25m investment he made to develop 150 apartments on Ipswich Waterfront – John still loves to buy and sell small sites and properties. He says, "It's great to be down at the coal face, dealing directly with people and doing it all yourself. The problem with the bigger deals is that it's not half as much fun, surrounded with advisors and consultants, so I still much prefer the smaller deals!"

John is also a regular participant on Property TV, appearing on *Property Question Time*, and he conceived and chairs the popular *Property Elevator* show.

He is a regular public speaker on property developing and investing, helping those entering the world of property dealing, or those who want to widen their property portfolios.

Following on from his first book, *John Howard's Inside Guide to Property Development & Investment*, this second book will extend your knowledge on putting a deal together, with step-by-step advice on converting properties and on handling listed and new build conversions. Guiding you through financial partnerships and back-to-back deals, John culminates with providing the right advice when dealing with other property dealers, leaving you hungry to do bigger deals and move up the investment scale.

FOREWORD AND ACKNOWLEDGEMENTS

Well, here I am writing the foreword for my second book in the *Property Developing & Investing* series, this time looking at how to do more sophisticated deals.

Since I wrote my first book last year, a lot has been happening: I've been asked to do numerous speaking engagements and to appear on radio and television, including a regular spot on Property TV within the series *Property Question Time*. I've also pitched two potential property shows to the channel, one of which has had the go-ahead to be made into a pilot show.

The people that have purchased my first book have made all of this possible. One lovely story was of a chap who bought a copy and enjoyed it so much, he then purchased a further seven copies for family and friends!

I've been asked by many people who have read my first book and heard me speak as to whether I will be putting together some seminars across the country – something that I will be delighted to do moving forward, so please look out for them. It will be a pleasure to meet you!

Thank you to everyone who has asked me to speak and to all of you that have either turned up to listen, or watched me on Property TV.

Once again, I would like to thank Vanessa Britton for helping me to write this book and, again, she has very kindly donated her fee to her Aim Higher charity, a school project in Africa for orphans and low-income families.

I very much hope you enjoy this book and I look forward to meeting you soon.

CONTENTS

INTRODUCTION

I'm hoping that you have previously read my first book, *John Howard's Inside Guide to Property Development & Investment* – in which I spoke about how to find property deals in the first place, – and have already enjoyed buying, selling, or investing. I trust that book helped you to gain confidence and not only gave you an insight into the world of property, but also some valuable advice, helping you to achieve increasing success with your deals so far.

I firmly believe that you never stop learning – even after 35 years in the business, I still take on new ideas. With this in mind, it's time to move on to more sophisticated deals.

You may not realise it, but by becoming a residential or commercial property developer, you will be helping to shape and improve society as a whole. At first, this might seem an odd statement to make, but it is true – without residential and commercial developers, there wouldn't be enough houses to live in, shops to sell food etc… the list goes on!

So, rather than being ambitious, greedy, ruthless people (as considered by a large proportion of the general public), in fact, in most cases, quite the opposite is true.

Without developers, every government would be in serious trouble when it comes to housing – whether it's the Conservative or Labour party in power, the Government desperately needs developers to build new houses and develop commercial space. Without this, no country can grow or improve the lifestyles of its citizens. Sadly, you only have to look at how some people are forced to live in third world countries, to see what happens when there is no development and to appreciate how fortunate we are here in the UK.

Rather than looking at property developers with disdain, society should be thanking them. These are people who have the ambition, drive and courage to make this country the wonderful place it is to live in today.

So, if you're not currently a developer, but are considering becoming one, or you are already within the circle, I hope you enjoy this book — and remember, wherever your journey takes you, be proud of your profession.

Right, let's get on with helping people!

JOHN HOWARD'S
INSIDE GUIDE TO
ADVANCED
PROPERTY DEVELOPING
& INVESTING

CHAPTER 1:
PUTTING A DEAL TOGETHER CORRECTLY WHEN PURCHASING

Those unfamiliar with the world of property developing may think that luck plays a big part and that deals often fall into your lap! Well, I'm going to explain why that it is definitely not the case!

Putting a deal together correctly takes time, effort and, in many cases, experience. In this chapter, I aim to help you through the process, saving you time and equipping you with the expertise required to get the deal done. Many potential deals fall by the wayside after a few weeks, because of over-expectation by the seller – who often just simply hasn't had the right information in the first place.

I will show you how I put deals together, always thinking one step ahead and anticipating any issues and problems that might arise during the purchasing process.

In most cases, it will be an estate agent that is selling the property. This can sometimes be a blessing, rather than dealing direct with the owner, in as much as that any blow you may wish to deliver to the seller can be softened by the agent. Don't worry too much if your message has been diluted somewhat, this will be the agent's way of trying to get both sides to agree to the deal. I've met few estate agents who like to deliver bad news to their client, so you can rest assured that they would do their best to deliver any information to them, with the intention of achieving the most favourable outcome.

The next thing to remember is, it's not where you start, it's where you finish and, along the way, there can be a number of ups and downs. The most important thing is to be in control of the deal from the start.

If you're using an agent, clearly your relationship with them needs to be excellent. They need to trust you and want to do business with you, more than they do with their existing client – who, in this instance, will be the person who will be paying them their commission.

It is totally unethical for an agent to receive commission from both parties and, these days, it's very rare that they will do so, however, making sure the agent knows they will be getting the re-sales from you should help greatly! Receiving the re-sales is pretty standard and, although most agents will realise this, it is still a good idea to confirm this in writing with them, prior to a deal being agreed with their vendor.

Remember that most agents are affable, confident people that appreciate positive feedback, so letting them know how pleased you are with their service and that you will not hesitate to recommend them to others will also get you in their good books – if it's true, even better!

Even if you have already agreed the price, the agent may let it slip that you could have bought it cheaper, or that the client has got problems, or other bits of information, all of which can put you in a stronger position and drive the deal in your favour.

Potential issues

Earlier, I mentioned anticipating any issues and problems that might come along. One example of this could relate to funding;

for instance, don't tell the vendor that you can exchange in seven days, when you know you can't. It may well be that you still need to drag the deal along for two months, but it's a lot harder if you are constantly being chased after the first seven days, rather than the first six weeks. In other words, in such a case, be clear that you need four to six weeks to exchange. Ideally, always under-promise and over-deliver!

Try to be as honest as possible when dealing with an agent. Of course, it could be that by revealing your full circumstances it may potentially put your offer to buy the property in jeopardy, if by telling the agent all the facts regarding your situation, they may well then advise their client not to issue you with a contract. So, do be careful what you say to them, especially if you only need a short period of time in order to sort out your funding, or you are about to exchange contracts on another property that will release cash to purchase this one.

Getting the contract issued to your solicitor is the most vital and important thing; it demonstrates commitment from the vendor that they wish to sell to you. When a contract arrives, I generally hope that my solicitor can find a few problems, which will delay any possible exchange – just in case I need more time to find the money.

If you can find a few issues, whether they are deal-breakers or not, don't reveal them all in one go; let the vendor know about the first one or two, then feed the rest in gradually. This will keep you in control of the deal – similar to when playing a game of squash; control the 'T' in the middle of the court and you will surely win the game!

If you need a delayed completion, for example, maybe in order to tie the purchase in with another sale, or to get your planning application in before you complete (to save time before you sell it on), don't inform the vendor about the delayed completion until your solicitor has sent them the 10% deposit.

If they know you are ready and willing to exchange, it will be much more likely that they will meet your demands.

If the vendor is not keen on the idea of a longer completion date, you could always offer them a deposit on exchange that is larger than the normal 10%, and also allow them to have the money straight away, instead of it sitting with their solicitor until completion. However, if you *are* going to offer this, make sure to check (via your solicitor) that they don't owe too much to their bank or building society, so that if they take the 10% deposit and spend it, they will be unable to pay off the loans.

Putting the deal together to sell

When it comes to selling the property on, the key is to be prepared, well before it has even been put on the market.

First of all, make sure that your solicitor has an up-to-date search from the local authority. This will stop any purchaser claiming "The search hasn't come back yet, so we can't exchange." It will also highlight any problems that have arisen since you purchased the property, which you may not be aware of. This way, you can head off any issues before they become a problem.

This search should then be included in the Legal Sales Pack, just as it would for a property auction. This will include a contract, alongside answers to standard enquiries from purchasers' solicitors – all prior to the property going on the market. If your solicitor objects to doing this, remind them that most of the work was done when you purchased the property, and a lot of it is just repetition.

When your solicitor assures you that they have prepared the Legal Sales Pack, always ask for a copy, so that you can check the contents. I've experienced situations where solicitors have said they've done this, only to find out that it has still taken a month for the purchasers to receive the contract – which is outrageous!

So, now you know you can get a contract to the buyer's solicitors easily within seven days of the sale being agreed, you are prepared to receive an offer. However, any timescale you put on the deal has to be from the time the buyer's solicitor receives the contract.

We will assume that you now have a proactive agent, who you can trust and who is acting in your best interests. If not, then quickly find another one that will!

Remember, when you inform the buyer that they have got 21 days to exchange from receipt of contracts, make sure that your agent believes it too. And definitely don't let the buyer know any more information than they need – such as if you desperately need to sell. Sharing this kind of information will only put you in a weaker position.

Having agreed the deal and the timescale, you need to make sure that the buyer has the funds to proceed. Ask to see proof of funds – make sure your agent confirms by email that they have either seen proof of the buyer's funds, or that the buyer can get a mortgage for the amount they require to purchase the property. Should the buyer be in a chain of house buyers, ask your agent to confirm that they have checked the chain thoroughly, and that all the buyers are in a position to proceed.

You are now in total control of the transaction. However, getting a buyer to this point is only 20% of the job – it's then down to the solicitors to make sure the rest of the process runs as smoothly as possible. Of course, deals that go through without a hitch and right on time are few and far between, so remember to be realistic. Try not to get disappointed or too frustrated – remember, the aim is to have the sale completed and the money transferred as soon as possible, so you can move on to the next bigger deal.

Preparation is key

So there you have it; if you follow the above advice, your property developing experience will certainly be easier than if you don't, and you will also have more control over the process. However, over the last 35 years, whether I've been doing small or large deals, there have been few transactions where people have said and done exactly what they say they would and within the time period agreed, so be prepared for every eventuality.

During any sales process, there are good days and bad days before the deal is completed. Remember, however, that often the bad days don't turn out to be as bad as first thought, while good days may not always be as good as they seem, so always keep your eye on the ball and be prepared to compromise when you need to.

Over the years, its rare that I haven't had to compromise in some shape or form, in order to get the deal done, and I believe it's a very brave person that is not prepared to do so — aside from the odd occasion when someone knows the deal is that good that they can afford not to compromise at all.

With this in mind, try to take the ups and downs in your stride and remember, however much humble pie you may have to eat to get there, the ultimate reward will be the money in your bank at the end of the transaction!

CHAPTER 2:
CONVERTING A BUILDING INTO FLATS – STEP-BY-STEP

In this chapter I'm going to take you through the complete building conversion process, from the first viewing of a property to the finished conversion – and the order in which everything has to be done.

1. Request a floor plan

Having viewed the property and decided it has potential to be converted into flats, the first thing to obtain from the vendor or agent selling the property is an existing floor plan. Hopefully, they will have one to scale.

If the seller doesn't have a floor plan, this can be an issue, as you will need to see one in order to calculate how to divide up the property. Luckily, most agents will supply a rough plan (not to scale) of the property details, which should be enough for you and your architect to work out what can be done with the building.

Once you have received the floor plan (whether full-scale or rough), you should email it to your architect. Ask them to provide a rough sketch of what they consider to be an acceptable scheme. Make sure that they put the actual size – in square footage or meterage – of each flat on the plans. Many people mistakenly think you can just work it out from the scale – well, I still can't after 35 years! Remember, you will probably need one parking space per flat, and possibly a few visitor spaces as well. Ask your architect to have this sketch back to you within 48 hours if possible. At this stage, as you have personally viewed the building and your architect has not, make sure that you agree with their proposed scheme, and that there is not an easier conversion possible.

2. Submit a pre-application enquiry

If you're happy with what your architect has proposed, ask them to prepare a pre-application enquiry to send to the local Planning Authority. In most cases, the authority will charge a small fee to deal with your application. A planning officer will make their recommendation to the Planning Authority, who will then make the final planning decision. They do usually take the recommendation of the officer so, happily, it is highly unlikely that the opinion will change. The Planning Authority can take up to 28 days to respond, but as you become more experienced, you will probably find that you are pretty sure of the outcome before they officially tell you. In any case, your architect should be able to advise you whether you will obtain planning or not, prior to the Planning Authority's official response.

3. Obtain quotes and valuations

While you wait for a decision from the Planning Authority, it's an ideal opportunity to bring in a builder to view the property and provide a quote for the conversion. They can also give you an idea of any problems that could arise during the project.

Next on the list is to get valuations from at least two estate agents for the flats on your draft plan. Remember to make sure that one of them is the agent who is selling the property – hopefully to you! You will stand a much better chance of buying it if they believe they will get the re-sales!

You will want to work out the sales/sqft price against other flats sold in the area – it's another way of checking the agent's advice. This information can be found online on the Government Land Registry site and on Rightmove, or similar property sites.

To do this, add up the room sizes for all the rooms in the property and divide it by the price it sold for. For instance, if the property is 1000sqft in total and it sold for £300,000, then that would be £300 per sqft sale price. This information is also really important when you wish to work out how much the builder is charging you for converting the building. Using the same size building as above of 1000sqft, if the builder charges you £100,000 for the conversion, then that would be £100 per sqft build costs. You can then compare these costs with those from other builders to make sure your builder is giving you a fair price.

If you find that an agent or builder quotes a build price for a flat without asking what the square footage or meterage is, then walk away and bring someone in who will cost accurately!

4. Make an offer

Once you have the rough cost of the conversion and you know what the sales prices are likely to be, you are then in a position to work out how much you can afford to pay for the building – in order to make the required 25% net profit after all costs (including bank interest).

If you know there are others interested in purchasing the same property, then it makes sense to put your offer in quickly, or to let the agent know that you intend to make an offer. (I'm assuming the agent who gave you the sale prices for the flats when developed is the same one who is selling the initial property, meaning, as I said earlier, that you clearly have a much better chance of sealing the deal).

If you think you know the outcome of the pre-application, then it's definitely worth making your offer. However, if there is a lot of interest, whether you know the decision regarding your pre-application or not, it is worth making an offer anyway. Even if you have to pull out at a later date, this means no one else can agree to buy it before you.

One thing to remember, however, when you receive the pre-application advice from the Planning Authority, at this stage, it is advisable not to show it to the agent; if you pull out at a later date, or reduce the price, the agent could use your pre-application to try and sell the property again to another client.

Property is all about risk and reward and it may be that you are able to make an offer subject to planning permission being granted, rather than having to buy without planning permission. This is a great situation to be in and I will discuss this in a later chapter, but clearly, the less risk you take on any transaction, the better. However, let's assume that this isn't the case on this occasion, but that you have had your offer accepted, solicitors are instructed, and the pre-application advice from the local authority is that you *should* receive planning permission, should you wish to put in an official application.

5. Submit a detailed planning application

Assuming your solicitor has had the search back and received the legal papers from the vendor's solicitor, it's time to start getting your planning application ready for submission. This should include a measured survey of the building and, of course, plans drawn to scale. You have two choices here; you can either go for an outline planning consent with little detail, which means you will have to submit details at a later date, or, if you are committed to developing the property, then I would suggest you go ahead with the detailed planning application – your architect will do this on your behalf before they start, so make sure you get a fixed price from them to include all working drawings.

Once you have submitted your planning application, you can follow its progress online on the local authority's planning portal, which is available to the public. This process should not take more than eight to 12 weeks. It's vital that you make sure that the architect who has submitted your application is pro-active and drives the application forward. They must enquire every seven to 10 days as to how the application is progressing and whether there is any further information required by the Planning Authority – if there is, make sure your architect submits this information within 24 hours. Remember, they are working for you and you are the one paying for it!

You should know fairly early on whether the planning officer dealing with the case is going to recommend your application for approval or not, or whether it needs to go to a planning committee. If there have been very few objections, then it's unlikely it will go to committee, it will just be written up as approved by the planning officer dealing with the case.

If, while reviewing the application, the planning officer decides something needs changing, remember, they are only doing their job, so it is always better to work *with* them. It may well be that your architect knows them well and will advise you accordingly, so don't be too stubborn – you certainly don't want a refusal because, for as long as you own the property and the work is not being done, it will be costing you financially (in empty rates, for example) and the less profit you're likely to make on completion.

Your application needs to be submitted on the day you exchange contracts. On no account should you submit it beforehand; if the sale falls through, you've then done all the work for the vendor, who can use the application to their advantage. Even if, legally, they're not meant to do this, all the information will be easily accessible on the local council's planning portal.

6. Create a schedule of works

Once you have submitted your application, you will then need to find a good building surveyor who can write a schedule of works for you. You can then pass this on to any builders you approach for the tender of the work, meaning they can all price the job based on the same information.

Your architect may try to persuade you that they can oversee the whole project. In my experience, they are very good at drawing up plans etc. and, in many cases, applying for planning permission, but they are generally not strong enough to deal with builders! Also, they quite often specify the use of materials that are at the more expensive end of the spectrum. You have to remember that, although very talented, most architects are not business people, their priorities often being that the building is aesthetically pleasing and that they can possibly win an award – exactly what you *don't* want, as it is likely to cost you extra money and may not make you any extra profit.

7. Put out to tender

Now you have your planning permission and a schedule of works, it's time to put your project out to tender – ideally to three builders; the one that you showed around initially and two recommended by your building surveyor. Agree a date with the builders by which they need to get their tender price back to you and stick to this date. You need to appear strong from the start. Even if a builder states that they can't meet this deadline, it is highly likely that they are just trying to gain an advantage over other builders.

I've heard a number of excuses in my time, as to why a builder can't provide their tender price by a particular date; the only one that generally turns out to be genuine is when they say that they are just too busy with work. In which case, if they're telling the truth, then they are probably not the ideal choice for the job, because they are likely to tender high as they don't need the work. You need a builder who you like and trust and, most importantly, whose previous work you have seen and who has been recommended by people you have spoken to.

8. Choose a builder

When it comes to reviewing builders' quotes, remember, it's not always advisable to go with the cheapest; if it's too cheap, they are likely to come back to you halfway through the contract with extra costs. Or, it may be a 'hospital job' – basically that they will fit the job in between other projects they are working on – meaning there is a good chance it won't be completed in time.

Always fit the builder to the job; don't choose a construction company that is a very large concern if you have a small job and, equally, don't choose a very small builder to do their first big job! Remember, you are much better off waiting an extra month to have everything fully organised and the right builder in place prior to starting, rather than finishing the job late – as further down the line, you will be at the highest point of the financial arch and paying a lot of bank interest.

Once you've chosen your builder, it doesn't hurt to check them out financially before you make a final commitment and there are ways you can do this online. At the end of the day, you are entrusting them with a very important building project, which must be delivered on time and on budget if possible.

A small piece of advice: when the builder informs you how long it will be before completion, it is prudent to add a further two months to this timescale, just to make sure you don't put yourself under any unnecessary pressure – of course, don't let the builder know you have done this!

9. Apply for building regulation approval

On any conversion project, you will also require building regulation approval for the works you are carrying out. Your building surveyor will be able to arrange this for you, or they will recommend another surveyor to do so on your behalf. Again, I would advise you not to use architects for this job, although they may well ask to provide this service. It is always better to use a specialist, someone who deals with nothing else but building regulation applications.

10. Obtain warranties

These days, you are well advised to provide a warranty for six to 10 years on the individual flats once they are completed. There are now a number of companies that provide this and your building surveyor will advise you accordingly. Make sure you arrange this well before construction starts. You can obtain retrospective warranties, but they are a lot more expensive as the company will not have been able to monitor and check the construction phases through to completion, so I wouldn't advise taking this route. Nearly all building societies will now insist on a warranty on any new build or new conversion, so make sure that you have one in place.

11. Submit utility applications

If you will be needing a new gas or electric supply, or any other utilities to do with the property, it is very important that you also get your applications for these in at this stage – there is nothing more frustrating than finishing the development and having no electricity, water etc., meaning you are unable to get a completion certificate from the local authority.

12. Check ongoing works and monthly valuations

As the project proceeds, the building surveyor will check not just the quality of the work, but also the builder's valuation on a monthly basis. This basically means that, each month, the builder will report how much work they have completed in that month and, therefore, how much money they require from the total building cost. Your building surveyor will make sure that the valuation is correct and that the builder is not claiming for more money than they are due. Sadly, it is all too common for builders to try to get as much money as they can during the early months, as it helps them greatly with their cash flow, so it is imperative for your building surveyor to be on top of this. The problem being that, if too much money is released too early, then, as the project nears its end, there will be very little money left for the builder to claim and little incentive for them to complete the project.

A good building surveyor will make sure that all monies paid to the builder throughout the project are correct, and will also have written a retention into the contract – normally 5% of the contract price – which the builder cannot claim until six months after the build work is completed, in case any issues need addressing.

13. Obtain completion certificates

You will need a completion certificate for each flat. The building inspector at the council – who will have visited the build on a regular basis as work has progressed – issues this. It can also be undertaken by other qualified private companies on a similar basis.

Make sure that these completion certificates, alongside electrical certificates and any guarantees given on things such as damp-proofing, timber treatments, boilers and any white goods you are putting in the kitchen, are all picked up by you and delivered to your solicitor. These are all extremely important and, as such, any purchaser will want and expect to have them. If you are installing gas central heating, then the boiler must also be registered with the local authority. I can't tell you how many times over the years I've had to chase builders for these certificates, or that they have been mislaid somewhere in the property!

14. Make a snagging list

When the builders inform me that the work is complete, I always take it that I'm a month away from actually having the building work completed to my satisfaction.

It is incredibly important that you make what is called a

'snagging list'. This is when you inspect the whole of your property meticulously and make a detailed list of anything that you feel has not been completed properly, which you can then give to the builder to remedy. Any good builder will have already carried one out, but always give each room an additional check yourself, to ensure that the condition and the finishes are to your satisfaction. There are bound to be a few things you are not happy with, but don't be disheartened, this is pretty standard and it generally takes at least two checks before you will sign off the work.

There is nothing that annoys me more than a builder who allows carpets to be fitted before work on the project has finished, and consequently getting them dirty. This will happen when a builder is late finishing the works and the carpet fitter is already booked in. To try and prevent this from happening, what I have done on occasion, is tell the builders that the carpets are coming two weeks earlier than they actually are, meaning they will hopefully work to a tighter schedule. Later, you can inform the builders that, 'out of the kindness of your heart', you have delayed the carpet fitters for two weeks to help them complete on time!

15. Market your property

When it comes to marketing your properties, don't be tempted to do this before they are finished (except, possibly, if the agent has a one-off viewer, where they think they may lose the buyer). It's vitally important that, for the first month of marketing, you have your show property looking pristine. I usually recommend holding a two-hour open session, to bring people in, create a buzz and give the impression that offers will be made. Don't be tempted to allow it to be open all day. It's not a shop! A shorter viewing time is much more likely to create an impact with prospective buyers.

Make sure that the builders have left nothing inside or outside the building, everything is clean and tidy, and that the garden and landscaping are all completed.

During the marketing of the flats, make sure that the gardens are kept tidy, with short cut grass and no weeds. Internally, make regular checks to ensure there is no damp and that the flats are not dirty or dusty, and pick up any mail. Personally, I always keep the heat on in all the flats, but low enough so as not to cause any condensation on the windows.

Many people are tempted to market their development before it is completed, but bear in mind that no one is going to complete the purchase of the flat until it's fully finished anyway, so you're not actually going to be wasting any time. However, do make sure you have the Legal Pack ready and waiting to go with your solicitors. That way, as soon as you find a buyer for a flat, this part will be already be completed, meaning the sale will go through quickly.

If you agree a sale early, then you have to be prepared for a buyer to start dictating what colour paint they want on the walls, or what type of kitchen they would like, or requesting other alterations to be made – all of which are time-consuming, not to mention often expensive. This is one of the main reasons why I don't recommend an early sale. It's much better to wait until further down the line, that way, if a buyer wishes to change anything, they can do so at their own expense after contracts are exchanged and before completion.

Of course, if you are developing a large number of flats or houses, the bank may well insist that you market some of the properties off-plan. However, be prepared for the possibility that these buyers may wish to resell the property prior to it being completed and at a profit – and employ a different agent than you to resell them, causing confusion in your marketing and potentially undercutting your own sale prices.

So there you have it, if you follow my advice, hopefully you will have achieved a successful conversion – and one that sells well.

CHAPTER 3:
CONVERTING LARGE COMMERCIAL BUILDINGS INTO RESIDENTIAL HOUSES AND FLATS

Over the course of my career, I have converted many types of properties into houses and flats – everything from large Victorian hotels, nursing homes and maltings buildings, to town halls, piggeries, barns and – probably one of the most unusual – a water pumping station.

Costs

The common factor with nearly all of these conversions is that they rarely came in on budget in terms of costs, or within the original time frame allocated. I've often managed to meet one or the other, but rarely both on the same development, so do remember to be cautious when pricing the cost of any project.

With a conversion, there are quite a few areas where the builder is unable to expose initially, so may not be able to give an accurate price until work has begun and they have a better idea of what the job entails. So, if the building is in a poor state of repair, one of the best ways to reduce the risk of this is to pay for a builder to do a sympathetic strip out, meaning the builder will expose all the areas of the property that are of concern. However, to ensure the builder only exposes the necessary areas, make sure your building surveyor provides the builder with a schedule of works prior to the strip out.

Because of the uncertainty surrounding the cost of converting existing buildings for alternative usage, it can deter many developers – especially those who prefer the security of a new build, where the project construction costs can be calculated pretty much to the penny. The good news is, however, that with this lack of competition from other developers, you should be able to look for a return in the region of 25% net of all costs and interest charges. With new builds, on the other hand, most developers will be happy to make 15% – and the large, national house builders often achieve even less than that (although some may have land banks – in other words, they have been purchasing land over many years, at a much lower cost than land that has been recently purchased and then developed, which, in turn, increases their margins).

As already mentioned, not only can a conversion be more difficult to price than a new build, in certain cases, it can also take longer to complete. This is because of the constraints of having to work around an existing building, rather than the 'blank canvas' of a new build, where work is carried out from the footings upwards.

Many believe that, because a building is already built and just needs refurbishing, then it should be a lot cheaper to do than a new build, but this all depends on the condition of the property. If it's in good condition and the work needed is minimal, then it will probably be a lot cheaper. However, if it is a complete redevelopment, do not be mistaken in thinking it will only cost you 50% of the cost of building new… because this almost certainly won't be the case! Yes, you will save money by the fact that it doesn't need building from scratch, but it will probably still end up costing you the same in time and money to repair as it would to build a new property.

As a very brief outline, in most developments the building costs are split 50/50 between the cost of labour and the cost of materials.

This can obviously vary somewhat, depending on whether or not there is a shortage of labour, or whether there is an increase in the cost of materials. As approximately 70% of materials are imported, this cost will also depend on the currency exchange rate at the time.

Stripping out

If the building is of historical importance and is therefore a listed property, you will need to be especially careful of what you have removed in a strip out. Before you commence with any removal, it is essential to get the permission of the Listed Building Officer at the local council. However, if, for any reason, you have not done so, then make sure that anything you do remove is stored, so it can be put back should the council require it to be. Also, be sure to take photographs of everything while the strip out takes place, to prove what was and wasn't there. We will discuss working with listed buildings in further detail later in this book.

After the strip out, you will have a better view of where any problems lie and how bad a condition certain areas are in. It shouldn't cost any more money overall as, at the start of any construction work, a strip out will be the first job to be done anyway. By bringing the strip out forward, you will know everything there is to know about the building before you start, resulting in an accurate cost quote from the builder.

Remember, once you have committed to a contract with your builder, if they then discover extra work that needs doing on top of the schedule of work agreed (because they just didn't know what was behind a wall you wished to remove, or the condition of a fireplace which is currently boarded over), you really have very little option but to allow them to continue – especially as they are already on site. The main problem being that they can then charge you however they see fit, as it will be considered an extra to the existing contract and so not priced up prior to the work commencing. At this point, you really are at their mercy, so the trick is not to get yourself in that situation in the first place!

You can see why early stripping out is so important, as this work will have to be undertaken anyway, I cant emphasise enough the importance of knowing as much as possible about a property, in order to be as accurate as possible when it comes to your build costs. One more point: even if you have thoroughly investigated the building prior to beginning the project, it is advisable to allow for at least a 10% increase in your costs as a contingency figure, in case something has been missed.

If the building has had commercial use, there should also be an asbestos report and it is essential that you see this prior to your purchase. This will reveal whether there is asbestos in the building and, if so, where and whether or not it needs to be removed. Make sure you get a price on any asbestos removal before you purchase the property as this can be extremely expensive.

Houses or flats?

When converting a building into a number of flats, work is traditionally completed from the top down, for the obvious reason that, once the first flat is finished, there will be no need to walk through it to work on the next one. The next thing to remember is that all tradesmen, such as plasterers, electricians, heating engineers, decorators etc., must be organised so as to complete their part of the job in the correct order – there is no point painting the walls if they still have to be re-plastered!

In my experience, when you're planning to convert a building into flats, one of the first things to consider is whether it will split naturally, with the minimum amount of structural alterations. Of course, the more structural alterations that you have to make, the more the development is likely to cost. Another thing to take into account is that, if when designing the internal layout of the conversion, it doesn't flow naturally and you find you have to force the design to make it work, it generally means that, in practice, it will also be harder to do and more costly to develop.

Generally, it costs less to convert properties into houses than it does flats. For starters, they split vertically into bigger units. Another obvious reason being that, rather than having two flats, with all the costs involved in having two of everything – heating boilers, bathrooms, kitchens etc. – you only need to budget for one of each. Costs for things such as soundproofing and fire precautions will also be less on a conversion to a house, as it's only the vertical walls between the next door accommodation each side that need to be sound and fireproofed on a house. You will have to do this between all floors and walls when it comes to converting a building into flats. In both cases, all sound and fireproofing needs to comply with building regulations.

Another advantage with converting into houses is that, if the property already has a number of staircases, it may be that it just splits naturally using one staircase per house. Even if you need to put an extra one in, it will certainly still be a lot simpler (and cheaper) than a flat conversion.

Converting existing offices into residential flats

Many office buildings have been converted into residential flats, especially since the Government has made it much easier to gain planning with the introduction of Permitted Development.

However, before you start, it is prudent to check whether the building is in a conservation area or not. If it is, you may well need to obtain planning. In any case, your architect should be able to advise you of what you can and cannot do.

Existing tenants

Having the right to develop office buildings is all very well, but if you cannot get vacant possession of the building, you are not going to get very far.

The first thing you need to do is to find out how long the occupiers have left on their lease. Secondly, you need to know whether the lease is inside what is known as the 54 Act (Landlord and Tenant Act 1954). This basically means that the tenant has the right to renew the lease on similar terms to the existing lease, should they wish to do so. If the lease is outside the Act, they are not. Even if it is inside the 54 Act, it may still be possible for you to avoid giving them a new lease if there is a clause within the lease for redevelopment. You will, however, have to prove that you wish to develop the building for an alternative use.

If the above is not possible, then it really is a case of negotiating with the tenant to gain possession – something I have had to do on numerous occasions! It is very important that you sit down face to face with the tenants and explain what your plans are. There is no point in stating that you want to do something different to that laid out in your actual plans – they will invariably see right through this and it is likely to destroy any chances you may have of a successful negotiation.

The main thing that will encourage any tenant to move is money. If you can help with relocation, then that is also a bonus.

The one trick you do have up your sleeve is that of dilapidation. If, within the lease, there is a clause regarding the condition of the premises, along with evidence by way of a Schedule of Condition as to what condition it was in when the tenant moved in, then there is a very good chance that, after a number of years of occupation, it will need a lot of money spent on it to get it back up to its initial condition. You can use this as a great negotiating point as, even though you have no plans of returning it to its original condition, it is likely to cost the tenant a substantial amount of money to do so when they finally vacate – a win-win situation.

Empty rates

One thing you do need to make sure of is that, by the time the building is vacant, you're ready to start work, because the empty rates on office buildings are extremely costly. Local authorities are very sharp at sending out rate demands and will not accept you stating that you're about to start work. They will need proof that the work has started, building regulations have been approved and the building is totally uninhabitable.

There are always companies who purport to be able to get around the law. Some may take a short lease off you and occupy the building as storage, charging as low as half of what the empty rates would have been otherwise.

Unfortunately, speaking from personal experience, on several occasions I have had to pay empty rates. One of my recent projects, an office, cost me £6,600 per month in empty rates until the builders officially started. I stripped out the building of all bathrooms and kitchens, making it legally uninhabitable, and argued that I should no longer have to pay these rates. Unfortunately, the rates department did not agree and we had to pay the monthly fee, which was costly. To avoid such costs, make sure that you have everything in place and a building contract awarded as soon as you can after you purchase the property.

Parking

Some people may shy away from developing if there is no parking area with the property. I have developed many buildings with no parking area, but the one good thing about purchasing these properties is that there is less competition when buying them. The downside, of course, is that it does put off a number of buyers once the building has been converted into flats. However, even when there are parking spaces, I sometimes find that having some parking, but not enough for every flat, can be more of a problem than having no parking spaces at all, because everybody wants a car space. Once every car parking space has been sold, the buyers that are left often feel that they have been short-changed and are disappointed.

I always research as to whether or not there is a car park nearby, where I can purchase 12-monthly permits — normally costing around £1,000 per year outside London. I then include a year's free parking with each remaining flat. If it's a multi-storey car park, then it can often be better than parking on site, because it's under cover and usually has 24-hour security coverage.

Developing higher storeys

If the office building has a flat roof, it may well be possible to develop that area into more flats, but bear in mind, construction for new flats on floors that are three or four storeys up is very costly — I've recently done this in Brighton and the cost came out at nearly 50% higher than the conversion rate of the other flats within the development.

Another thing to watch out for is when agents state that top floor flats will be penthouses, so will command a higher figure per square foot than the rest. They may have better views and a lift, but check the square footage and also the head height of the flats; you may well find that they only have full head height in the middle of the rooms and that the sides and the two ends have sloping ceilings, so you are unable to stand up fully in those areas.

I would always sacrifice a portion of internal space in order to create a balcony on the top floor flats and, if you can do two balconies, even better – one from the lounge and one from the master bedroom.

Appearance

Lastly, it is very important that the building no longer looks like an office building once the conversion is complete – there is nothing worse. There are some reasonably cheap external facades available that you can install, which will transform the look of the building, but make sure your architect has some flair – if they don't, bring someone else in to help with this. Most importantly, *always* make sure that any external facades or cladding you choose meet all fire safety standards. It is always better to spend a little more to guarantee this is the case.

In summary, although it may seem like a lot to remember, don't be deterred from doing a conversion. Over the years, I have made more out of conversions than any other type of property development. Just make sure that you do your investigation on the building and strip out, prior to getting a final building cost estimate from the builder. It's better than disagreeing with builders over how much more you owe them for the extra work they have carried out, or worse still, work stopping on the site altogether – neither of which you want to contemplate! Remember, it's far better to take your time at the initial stage, than to rush in, find yourself in a muddle, and end up losing control of the costs and, ultimately, the development.

CHAPTER 4:
LISTED BUILDING
CONVERSIONS

If you believe that the average developer shies away from converting existing properties, preferring the easier job of new build, then it stands to reason that listed buildings will be even more unpopular. However, I say... no guts, no glory! Personally, I've made far more money out of Grade 2 listed properties than those that aren't listed. The reason being that there is far less competition when you come to buy, due to the complexities involved when purchasing buildings with historical importance.

There are three different types of listing, depending on the historical importance of the building along with the merit of its architecture:

Grade 2 – A Grade 2 building is the easiest listed building to develop. Generally, changes to the look of the outside are not permitted at all, but you may well be allowed to split some rooms up internally – however, you're likely to have to keep the staircases as they currently are. I have managed to get permission to block staircases up in the past, but never to remove completely, on the basis that, at a future date, they can then be reinstated. Having said that, I *have* been allowed to put in new staircases. A similar premise applies to the splitting of the rooms, in that, at some point in the future, they could be put back to the original size should someone wish to do so.

There may be an occasion whereby the building inspector (who must work to building regulation standards) disagrees with the Listed Building Officer, who, in turn, may not allow certain works to be carried out. Generally they will come to a compromise, but in certain cases, the Listed Building Officer will have jurisdiction over the building inspector.

Grade 2 Star – I have developed a number of these buildings. English Heritage have to be involved when developing Grade 2 Star buildings and will advise the local authority, in conjunction with the council's Listed Building Officer, as to what alterations and modernisation will be acceptable. You are also likely to need a historian to produce an historical report for each room in the building. I recently converted a Grade 2 Star building into seven apartments and the historical report that was carried out cost me £10,000, so this type of building conversion definitely brings with it more restrictions than a standard Grade 2.

Grade 1 – A Grade 1 listed building is incredibly difficult to convert. Throughout my career, I have only done one of these, and I have no inclination to do another one, as it was fraught with complications. For one thing, I was not allowed to put a kitchen in a certain room. Despite agreeing not to attach it to any wall, so it was freestanding – it still wasn't acceptable. My advice is not to get involved in developing any Grade 1 listed building unless you wish to live in it yourself.

Remember, when looking to convert Grade 2 Star or Grade 1 listed buildings, you need the consent of English Heritage and have to produce extra reports. Because of this, it will take you much longer to obtain planning permission to develop such properties. Once you have planning permission, you will also need listed building consent – normally applied for and granted concurrently with your planning permission

You can, of course, employ your own historical expert to challenge any decisions made by a Listed Building Officer – regarding works that they will not allow you to carry out – on the basis that their research, and, therefore, their decision, is flawed, or that by not allowing such work, the building will not be restored. At the end of the day, it has to be a compromise and balance between allowing work that will make the project financially viable, and historical restoration for future generations to enjoy. However, employing such tactics can delay the start of your development even longer.

The best advice I can give you is to invite the Listed Building Officer to view the building with you early on when you just have the draft plans, seek their advice and do your best to work with them. The whole point of granting permission to develop and convert such buildings is that it helps to retain and preserve them for the future. It is always good to remember this when negotiating – and be prepared to compromise.

During the process, if you have any worries about removing anything structural from the building, make sure you take photographs of everything. Also, retain everything you do remove, just in case the listed building officer disagrees with your decision – in which case you can obviously put it back. There are massive fines and, ultimately, prison sentences for people who do not abide by the law when it comes to developing historical buildings.

However, as previously stated, the good news is that you should have a lot less competition when buying listed buildings, compared to any other type of property. But having said that, you must also appreciate that the building costs will be higher than normal. It is a widely-held belief that the property can be sold for more money as it has character and history, however, in my experience, the benefit of living in an historical building is often outweighed by the fact that it needs more maintenance and by the amount of permissions required in order to make any changes – right down to agreeing the colour of paint on the externals of the building.

CHAPTER 5:
NEW BUILD

There is a good reason why I haven't done a huge amount of new build development over the years, and that's because there are usually builders that can build them cheaper than I can; builders who have physical involvement on site, saving on labour costs by doing the work themselves, or by organising the labour directly – something I don't have the ability to do.

However, the good news is that, as well as being able to build cheaper, such builders can also afford to pay more than I can, so even if I find a development site which is not worth my while building out, it doesn't mean that I can't still sell it on at a profit.

If the site consists of around 10 houses or more, then the builder's costs are likely to be much closer to mine, as they will be unable to do as much of the work themselves and are likely to tender out a percentage of the work just as we would. If it's a very large site, I really do have to employ one of the bigger builders to develop it and they will charge me the same as they would anyone else.

However, although I don't personally favour new build development, there are many property developers who began by building just one house and ended up becoming very large house-building companies, such as Barrett Homes, for example!

So, if new build development is what interests you and you

have experience in one of the building trades or with digging foundations, then this route is clearly right for you.

The build

The great thing about new build is that, as long as you do extensive initial research and work out all the costs, you know exactly how much it will cost you to build – there really should be no extras!

Many builders will use the services of a quantity surveyor, whose job it is to estimate the cost of the works to be carried out. Make sure you are provided with a Full Bill of Quantity, which will contain information such as how many bricks or roof tiles need to be purchased etc. My experience of quantity surveyors, however, is that they will often estimate on the higher side, with the intention of reducing the risk of being sued for pricing a job too cheaply – consequently, this is one of the few occasions I am likely to reduce the quoted cost by 5%.

Before you begin any new build project, you need to make sure that all permissions required are in place and that you know the full cost of the build. You will also need to ensure that all utilities will be available; water, gas, electricity and mains drainage. These must be organised well before you start work on site, as the relative services will probably need quite a lot of lead-in time before installation.

The time of year is also an important factor with any build. You want to begin the ground works while the land is relatively dry, and always aim to get the roof on by September/October, after which the weather often deteriorates – you don't want to have building work exposed during the winter months of the year.

As recommended previously for conversions, for new builds you will also need a 10-year insurance-backed building warranty, provided by one of the national companies. If you don't have these, you are highly unlikely to be able to sell the completed properties to anyone who has a mortgage – and as this is probably 80% of purchasers in the UK, the risk is just not worth taking!

Most new builds will take around nine months to build. Even if you are told it will only take six, you still have to factor in landscaping, fences and driveways. Also worth noting is that, if the access is off a public road, there are only certain companies that are permitted to install dropped curbs. You are unlikely to be allowed to do this work yourself – the local authority will usually have a list of approved contractors.

The finish

Regarding the finish of the properties, there are a few important points to be aware of:

- Broadband is now the number one issue for purchasers, so make sure that you check early on what services are available in the area, and do whatever you need to do to install the strength required.
- Whatever you do, don't get carried away with kitchens. Kitchen manufacturers can vary greatly. In regard to costs, as a general rule, I will only spend 2% of my sale value on kitchens. So, in a £500,000 house, I will spend £10,000 on the kitchen – this is a really good discipline and will stop you, or any interior designer, from overspending. I recently heard about a developer who spent £50,000 on the kitchen of a house worth £600,000, which is total madness! I also work on the same 2% cost basis for bathrooms – and don't let anyone tell you that is not enough for two bathrooms and a cloakroom, because I can assure you that it is.

- As the landscaping is usually the last thing to be completed on any build, by this point in time, many people will have already gone over budget and consequently think that they can get away with spending very little on this. In my opinion, however, you do need to invest a decent amount in the landscaping. It can often be the first thing a buyer sees, so it needs to look sharp. You must make the first impression a good one as it will set the tone for the rest of the viewing, and give the buyer confidence that the rest of the build will be of a similar standard. Ensure you install decent quality patios, footpaths and fencing, and turf green areas as this will give instant impact, compared to grass seed.

Selling off-plan

With new build housing, it is a lot easier to sell off-plan, as opposed to selling conversions, which really have to be completed before you can put them on the market. With a good estate agent in place, once you know you are starting to develop the site, there is no reason why you can't take some reservation fees for the properties. It may be that you can even persuade some of the buyers to exchange contracts at this stage, proving total commitment to the purchase.

If you do decide to sell off-plan, before informing any buyer of a completion date, make sure you have given yourself ample time to fully finish the properties. There is nothing worse than being put under pressure, week after week, by buyers who are desperate to move in, and the house is still not completed. I've known of buyers who have already sold their own properties and have then had to move into temporary accommodation because the builder hasn't finished their new house. Remember, no one can move into a newly developed house until it has been issued with a completion certificate, and no building society will allow their borrowers to complete the purchase with you until you have supplied one.

Purchasing new build sites can be very competitive, being a fairly straightforward form of property development. Because of this, the profit margins are generally not that high. Most house builders will work towards a 15% net profit. However, if you can look to buy sites subject to planning, or sites that you initially promote and subsequently go on to purchase, then you can increase your margins significantly – making new build very worthwhile, even if you are paying other building companies to construct the sites for you.

Remember, if you're not building houses yourself – 'getting your hands dirty' on site and constantly looking after your workforce – then you will have much greater opportunity to search for other sites to purchase.

CHAPTER 6:
FINANCIAL PARTNERSHIPS

Financial partnerships work best where each party is contributing something different. If you both do exactly the same thing, in my view, there seems little point in getting together and just doubling up on everything.

Throughout my career, my partners have been essential to my ambitions. Without these people – most of whom I'm still working with, over 30 years later – there is no doubt that I would have been less of the success that I am today. They have also taught me a great deal along the way.

In my case, it's always been my job to find the deals, do the deals and sell on. I'm assuming that, as you're reading this book, you are in a similar position and what you're looking for is a financial partner. Ideally, this will be someone who is not going to get too involved in the actual deals, as that will be your department.

Gaining trust

With any financial partner, it is essential that you gain their confidence from the start. The chances are that they will be the one putting in the cash, while you are bringing the expertise, so always start off with a small deal to gain their trust and confidence – don't be tempted to run before you can walk. Finally, *never* over-promise and under-deliver, *always* under-promise and over-deliver – that way, the confidence in you will increase and the second deal you do with them is likely to be a lot bigger than the first.

If at all possible, try not to take any money out of the deal until the end of the transaction when the profits can be shared. If my financial partner is funding the project, I will usually take between 30% and 50% of the net profit, after they have received all their money back and interest on the investment.

Knowing your role

The part played by the financial partner in any deal is to arrange the funding and put up the cash necessary to do the deal. As explained earlier, my part is having the expertise to find the deal, do the deal and make a profit, but I always make sure that I keep my financial partner informed throughout the process – after all it's likely to be their money invested in the project.

If your financial partner could do the deal themselves using their own money, then they wouldn't need you and, as finding deals is usually not their forte, you are as important to them as they are to you. Sometimes I am asked why I think I deserve up to 50% of the profit and my answer is simple; without me there is no deal!

As extra reassurance to any financial partner, I always guarantee to pay my share of any loss incurred, should there be any. However, I do not put any money into deals with partners – using it instead to fund deals with my own property companies.

In my experience it's not essential to be friends with your financial partner. You may become friends over time, but they are likely to be business friends rather than personal friends, which is somewhat different. I never let myself become too involved on a personal basis with my backers, even when, in some cases, I may have known them for many years.

The truth is that, if you are active in the property market, it's virtually impossible to have enough money to do all the deals you wish to do. As opportunities arise, sometimes you will have funds available to invest yourself, and sometimes your money will be tied up in other projects – this is why partners are so important. Just remember that any partnership needs to be agreed on your terms as much as theirs. If either party is not happy, then things will deteriorate as the project develops. If any problems arise, make sure they are dealt with before you begin the project, otherwise it will be a lot harder – and more expensive – to sort out once there are profits to share at the end of the deal. Unfortunately, if issues are left unresolved, there is invariably only one winner – the lawyer!

CHAPTER 7:
PLANNING PERMISSION

Buying property subject to planning permission

When it comes to buying subject to planning permission, I almost see this as a 'free hit'! What I mean by this is that there's often a way of getting out of the deal should you not want to proceed – maybe it's not as good a deal as you originally thought – even after you have committed to signing the agreement

There are ways of manipulating the planning permission, so that you don't have to purchase the property, even if you have obtained planning. Perhaps the market has gone down, or you don't have the funds you thought you were going to have, or maybe you bought it subject to planning, with the belief that you could sell it on to someone else once this came through, *before* you had to pay for it – something I occasionally do.

If you are in a position where you don't have enough money to purchase a site, but you are able to raise the deposit needed to exchange contracts subject to planning permission (I normally offer 5% on that basis, rather than the traditional 10%), you can still go ahead with the deal, because it's likely to take anything from six to 12 months before you complete and have to hand over the remaining funds, due to the fact that you have to obtain the planning permission.

Withdrawing from a deal

When your solicitor is working on the legal agreement with the other party, make sure they get confirmation that they understand that any planning permission granted would be subject to your satisfaction. This basically means that, if you don't like the planning permission you eventually obtain, you are able to withdraw from the transaction and get your deposit back. This is the simplest and safest way of cancelling a deal should you not wish to proceed. Alternative options would be to withdraw the application at some point during the planning process, indicating that you no longer wish to proceed, or to make sure that the planning permission that you eventually apply for is not going to be acceptable to the local authority, meaning that your application will be refused. Any of these options will allow you to legally end the transaction and have your deposit returned.

Positivity and profit

Now I've explained how you can get out of a deal, for whatever reason, it's time to be positive – any property you can agree to buy, without having to complete the purchase before increasing its value, has got to be very good news indeed. Lets look at an example: you agree to purchase a piece of land, where the owner believes there is a possibility of planning permission for two houses, and it is offered you on that basis for £150,000. However, you then discover that you can actually get four houses on the land and so it is then worth £250,000 to a builder to build out the properties. If you can sell it to the builder on the same day as purchase, then clearly you can make £100,000 profit instantly. This will obviously be less any costs, including your initial 5% deposit (£7,500) and the cost of obtaining planning (usually around £ 10,000) – of course, if you can get the builder to pay for the planning permission as part of the deal, you will save yourself this £10,000.

Not all deals go to plan, hence it's really useful to have the ability to get out of it should you need to. One thing to remember is that, when agreeing a deal subject to planning permission, you're not committed to a certain number of units in that agreement. Don't be coerced into stating an exact number of properties, instead, always have the flexibility to build more units on the site should you wish to. However, try to get this flexibility fixed in the agreement, without the owner of the land being able to benefit from you any further. When an existing owner tries to put a legal requirement on you to share any uplift you may have in the number of properties you manage to build on the site – either now, or in the future – it is sometimes described as an overage. Avoid this at all costs, as it can cause a lot of legal complications should you build more properties on the site and wish to sell it on – it will certainly have a detrimental effect on the value you can get.

If you're initially entering into the world of property development with a minimum of funds, this is clearly a great way to start – and continue – as outlaying very little for a large return is an attractive proposition for any property developer, whether it's your first foray into business, or you are a seasoned campaigner such as myself. Anybody would be proud of being able to do a deal such as that outlined above and, over the years, I have completed many like this – they are great fun!

In my opinion, if you have the chance of a 'free hit' and of getting planning, always go for it, purely for the fact that you can get out of it should you not wish to proceed.

Make sure that the application you make to the local authority is on the basis of outline planning permission only, and not detailed – for a number of reasons: it will be quicker to put in your application and so get a decision; it will be cheaper; plus, most builders whom you sell on to will have their own particular view on what style of house they wish to build, and may even believe they can get a more suitable planning permission than you have. If they feel they have done better for themselves, then they will often be more inclined to buy from you in the future, should you contact them with another deal. It is always worth leaving a little in it for the next person, after all, 'there is nothing sweet in nothing'.

Obtaining planning when buying land

Unless you are a builder yourself, or enjoy getting physically stuck into a project, always let contractors build your new houses – they can almost certainly build them up to 20% cheaper than you will be able to. Your job is to go out and find more deals, so let someone else do the hard graft.

However, this doesn't mean you shouldn't be buying land in order to get planning, or if its already got planning, because you think you can change the style or density, increase the number of houses, or change into flats – and then sell it on again. This is smart developing!

You may have heard that the Government is currently pushing very hard to make it easier to obtain planning permission for residential properties, having realised that there is a massive shortage of housing across the UK – especially in the south – and that only half of the houses required per annum were actually being built. This can partly be put down to the fact that the top 10 house builders in the UK control a lot of the land and only choose to build a certain number of properties, in order to protect the prices they get – its all about supply and demand!

It is easy to get carried away with this government intention, however, what they propose and what actually happens on the ground are sometimes two very different things. In my opinion, most councils are still largely against developing land for housing and often make you fight all the way – you're certainly not pushing an open door – so please bear this in mind when you are looking to obtain planning permission.

These days, there is less risk when it comes to buying land, as you can now apply for what is known as a pre-application from the local authority. Although the risk is reduced, this has somewhat taken the fun out of purchasing new sites; you apply to the planning officer stating your intentions for the land usage, and they have to respond to it within 28 days. You can sometimes be charged for this, but if you get a favourable response, it is worth the fee as you are likely to obtain the planning you require. Please note, however, that when you receive your initial response, this is only the personal opinion of the planning officer, not the planning committee, so remain a little cautious – especially if the planning officer has only just qualified!

Do your research

Before you decide to purchase any piece of land, always do your research! I have seen cases where someone gets to an auction, discovers a piece of land seems to be going very cheaply, sticks their hand up and buys it – only to find out afterwards that every avenue regarding obtaining planning permission has already been exhausted to no avail! Just because you think you should get planning, doesn't mean you will. For example: I have just been turned down on a plot of land I was hoping to develop as a joint venture with a farmer in Buxton. On inspection, it looked a great site and one that would require a simple planning situation, but we were refused on appeal, due to the fact that it would look different to the people walking down the footpath at the side of the site – it clearly would and they wouldn't like it! That argument, of course, could be made about most development sites – it just depends on what planning inspectorate you get on appeal.

Appeals

When it comes to appeals, if it's only a small development, I would recommend that you submit a written appeal. This is a lot cheaper than organising a meeting on site on your behalf between your architect, planning barrister and planning consultant, and the planning inspector. The inspectorate is appointed by the Government to consider your appeal. Approximately 50% of appeals are upheld, so if the planning application fails, but your advisor (via the planning consultant, or architect) thinks it's worth appealing the decision, then it probably is. The appeal process takes approximately six months.

Planning officers

There are a number of ways in which you can increase your chances of being successful with your planning application, so it doesn't end up going as far as an appeal.

The first thing is to be realistic about what you plan to build on the site. Don't try to take the planners on like some triathlon challenge, instead, try to work with them. If you get permission to build slightly less than you were thinking you could on the site, but without any planning hassle, and you feel it could still make you a good profit, then accept it, thank them very much and get it sold!

Usually a specific planning officer will be assigned to your case. Unfortunately, after gaining experience with councils, it seems that, these days, all the best planning officers seem to be heading off into private practice – sometimes as a planning consultant against the council, or dealing with other aspects of planning.

This is a dreadful shame and seems to have predominantly come about because councils tend not to pay their best planning officers an appropriate salary – and these planning officers have massive workloads and are constantly under tremendous pressures to perform. I recently met with the latest government minister in charge of planning and shared my thoughts on the current planning system.

Unfortunately, since 2010, there have been numerous planning ministers in government, which has not helped when it comes to sending out a consistent message.

I will always try to avoid dealing with planning officers who have just come out of university and have little or no experience. Obviously, they try to do their very best, but a good planning officer needs to be able to call on his own life and planning experience in order to provide beneficial advice and make competent decisions. I don't particularly relish the idea of my livelihood being decided by someone who has little or no knowledge and needs time in the job to gain the necessary experience. If you are unhappy, because you feel you are dealing with a young, inexperienced planning officer, I suggest you contact the chief planning officer of the council as soon as possible and explain the situation to them. I completely understand that any good planning officer has to begin their career path at some point – just not with one of my applications please!

Meeting the locals

Before I submit any planning application, I will always arrange a meeting with the local parish council chairman to discuss my plans and, hopefully, gain their support. Although the council can ignore the opinion of the parish, I do believe that if you can get them on your side, it can only help. Even if they feel they can't support your proposal in its current form, the chairman might have suggestions which could make it much more appealing; it might be that they need help with some community fundraising, or a new playground etc. Apart from anything else, it displays good manners, along with respect for the parish in which you are trying to get planning permission. As I said before, it can't do any harm.

Technological advances

One good thing that's come out of recent technology is that each planning authority now has a planning hub, containing each application, along with all the up-to-date plans and files, so anybody can see at what stage the application is at – this is incredibly useful.

In the past, if you wanted to see a new or existing planning application, you had to physically go to the council offices, where they would give you the file to sit and read, but it could not be taken from the building and had to be returned before you left.

Architects

When getting planning permission for a house, you should consult with an architect; these people are extremely intelligent and patient – it takes seven years to qualify as an architect! However, as I mentioned earlier in this book, although an architect is very good at doing what they do, they are certainly not the ideal choice of consultant in other areas. Do not let your architect get involved in overseeing the construction, or dealing with the builders or other trades – this is not why they spent seven years at university and, besides, they are probably far too well-mannered to to be dealing with builders on a daily basis.

When choosing an architect, the first thing I will usually ask them is how many awards have they won. Ten minutes later, after they have finished enlightening me, I will tell them straight that they probably won't be winning any awards working for me! To be honest, in my opinion, most of the awards given are for over-designed, flamboyant buildings – usually at great cost to their clients – and I have no interest in boosting architects' egos or their bank balances.

A good architect should be able to assess the situation and design something complimentary to the area, that meets the budget and what the market requires, and allows the client to be able to resell it at a good profit! If your architect can't manage this, because they are working to their own agenda, find a new one – there are plenty about. This may sound as if I'm not fond of architects; the truth is, I am – but only of the good ones!

One such man was my great friend Rodney Furze, sadly no longer with us. He told me, when I started working with him over 30 years ago, that he didn't need to win any more awards. In his later years, he returned to university to study Greek architecture and was also made a Doctor of Architecture – a fantastic achievement. He was a wonderful man and architect, who was still doing smaller projects for us right up until the time he died, aged 87.

Planning consultants

The role of the planning consultant has really grown in importance over the last few years, and this is all due to the complex nature of the planning laws in this country. The architect alone can no longer keep up with all the planning laws, appeals etc. If you have a tricky application, it is worth speaking to a planning consultant who is not an architect, but who probably has a degree in planning law – they will work alongside an architect in order to advise him on the current planning laws. If the planning application looks like it's going to encounter difficulties, you will invariably require a planning consultant.

Remember, throughout the whole planning process, you are the one that needs to drive things forward. The consultants you are using are usually very busy, so if you don't maintain contact, you are likely to slip to the back of the queue. The same goes with the planning officer at the council; if you're dealing with them directly, chase them up regularly in a pleasant, non-threatening way. If you have instructed your architect or planning consultant to act on your behalf, then make sure they do the work – keep chasing them and get answers. Try to work to a timescale that they say is possible from the start and make sure they confirm this by email, after all, you may have borrowed money on the deal and be accruing interest – time is money!

Costs associated with planning

There are a number of costs associated with getting planning permission on land, and it's very important to include them in your financial equation – there is no getting out of these fees.

Planning application fees have to be paid upon submitting the application. Your architect should provide you with a fixed price on the fees for the application, and make sure this also includes chasing up the application while it's going through the planning process. Some architects may state that the fee is purely for submitting the application, but this is only half the job done. Make sure that you always agree a fixed fee with your professionals, rather than an hourly rate, and always get this confirmed in writing.

Planning law is constantly changing; most recently in the case of the Community Infrastructure Levy (CIL), which has replaced the previous Section 106 contributions – although some councils are still yet to adopt the CIL. Your advisors should explain this, but basically, it's a contribution that you make towards things such as education and playground facilities that the council have to pay for. Whether your council still has the Section 106, or the new CIL, you will still have to make these payments, so please check and make sure you are aware of the total costs.

Social housing

On top of this, you may also have to meet the social housing requirement that is now expected by most councils. I could write a book on this subject alone, but what I will say is, be aware of this and ask your advisors what the implications will be for all fees, including those regarding social housing. Do your research thoroughly if you wish to avoid the social housing requirement – for instance, rather than building social housing on the site, you may well be able to negotiate a commuted payment, which is a financial payment made by you towards building social housing in another area.

Land surveys

There are other things that also need to be checked with any land purchase: the ground conditions with a possible contamination report, together with a topographical survey, habitat survey and a possible archaeological dig. However, this last one is reasonably unlikely and won't need to be done unless the council believe there has been some historical interest on the site in the past. Your advisors should advise you prior to an application going in.

In partnership with another developer, I recently acquired a site of 1.75 acres, consisting mainly of buildings and a car park

Having done some research prior to the purchase, I discovered it was the former garden of Thomas Wolsey. The initial estimates of the cost of the archaeological dig (which is a legal requirement) on the site were in the region of £500,000. I arranged permission, so that we could dig some trial trenches in the car park, and found nothing of importance prior to the purchase. However, once the demolition had been concluded, there was a further archaeological dig over the whole site, where a number of items from the Saxon age were found, the final cost being in the region of £350,000. We also demolished the office building, only to find that the 1960's building that was there previously had been buried beneath the new building and that it was full of asbestos. The cost of removing this hazardous substance was an extra £300,000, which just goes to show, whether you have 40 years experience or not, not all developments go to plan.

If you own the land and wish to sell it, rather than obtaining planning permission yourself, an option would be to allow the person who is interested in purchasing your property the opportunity to apply for planning permission and then buy the land from you subject to planning being granted. However, if you choose to do this, it is imperative that you insist on a tight timeframe in which they must obtain planning – in my experience, this should be no more than six months.

CHAPTER 8:
TRADING DEALS

I have probably gained more of a reputation for trading deals than for developing sites to completion and many people are under the impression that it's a very glamorous life buying and selling property – that property developers spend every day doing so, and all are multi-millionaires! Unfortunately, this is far from the truth.

Yes, of course, I am constantly on the look out for great deals, but it may surprise you to know that, only last year, I bought nothing in 10 months because the market was difficult. I won't lie, it can be difficult to remain disciplined and keep your money in your pocket, but if you feel the market isn't right, or you're just not finding deals that are good enough, this is exactly what you need to do.

It's incredibly easy to buy for the sake of buying, especially if you're someone who likes to always have deals on the go.

Just as a football striker may go through a spell where they can't hit a barn door, then has a run where every shot finds the net, as a property developer, you have to be prepared to take the rough with the smooth. Try not to get disheartened when things don't go well and you can't find any deals, but likewise, be careful not to become over-confident and arrogant when it seems that everything you touch works out. Always be suspicious if, every time you make an offer, it is accepted, as this is not a normal scenario. It could be that the market is moving down and you just haven't realised as quick as others have. As the saying goes, 'form is temporary, class is permanent', so always believe in yourself and your ability – and the ability of your team to find you the best deals. And if you feel that members of your team are not making the grade, then find others who will!

A simple example of this would be where you purchase a house in poor condition, but with a large side garden with planning potential. Erect a fence along the side of the property, thereby splitting the potential plot at the side away from the main house. This way, you can put the house alone straight back on the market, while keeping ownership of the extra piece of land. You can then apply for planning permission on the side plot that, once granted, allows you to sell it separately – a simple way of adding value to your original purchase.

I am always on the lookout for deals that consist of more than one element – it might be a house with an office building or some spare land at the back – so I can split the site up and sell parts off individually, hopefully bringing in significantly more revenue than the cost of my original purchase.

Of course, the larger the site, the more potential there is to separate for re-sale. I have had great success by doing this over the years. As you become more well known as a dealer, people will be aware that you sell properties on at a profit immediately after purchase, so will come to you directly, or through an active agent.

These days, it's very easy to find out the price paid for a property. Personally, I always inform any buyer what I paid initially and my selling price. This way, they are aware of all the facts and can make an informed choice as to whether they still wish to buy my property. If you are not forthcoming with this information, and the buyer finds out before exchange of contracts, they will nearly always try to reduce the price, so

I like to deal with this issue at the start – before I commit to selling to them and end up wasting a lot of my time.

Being a 'deal junkie' is great fun, but it is always best to buy with the intention of developing the site out. Be disciplined. On the few occasions that I have bought property thinking that I'll just sell it on quickly as it is not worth my while developing it, that's when I have usually become unstuck. Always make sure you're buying for the right money and be prepared to develop it out if you find you can't trade it out – and assume that's exactly what you will have to do. Whatever you do, make sure everything stacks up before you make your purchase.

CHAPTER 9:
LAND PROMOTION

Land promotion has become a popular choice for landowners who have no planning experience and who do not wish to take the financial risks involved in applying for planning permission themselves. How it works is that the landowner decides to sell the land for development and is prepared to give away up to 30% of the value of the land to the developer – once planning permission has been obtained and the land has been sold on – but it is the developer who will fund the application for planning permission, and therefore be the one taking the financial risk, should it not be granted.

For a prospective developer, who maybe hasn't got enough money to purchase any property, land promotion provides a real chance to make a substantial profit, should they choose the right site to promote. It's an opportunity seriously worth investigating and could give you a great start in the world of property developing!

I've recently become involved in a number of land promotion deals, where I've taken the risk and outlaid my money in order to obtain planning permission. The reason being that, as most people are aware, there is an incredible housing shortage in the UK, meaning the Government has given every local authority five-year targets, with regards to how many houses are being built.

Local authorities, especially in the south, are under incredible pressure to release land for housing. This has given property developers a unique window in which to drive through planning sites that, in the past, may never have been accepted for house building. Part of the reason why many local authorities are vulnerable to this action, is that they have not managed to convince the Government that they have a five-year housing supply that is deliverable.

I will now take you through the process I use to evaluate whether or not I wish to take a financial risk – anything from £20,000 on a small site to £200,000 on larger sites – and gamble on whether I will get planning on a site that I don't own. When I say gamble, however, it's really more of a calculated risk, as I will use my experience, my planning consultant's advice and my gut feeling to decide whether or not I will be successful. Some take the view that if they invest in enough sites, just through sheer numbers, they are likely to be successful on some! Personally, I take a slightly more cautious view and evaluate every site on an individual basis. If I don't feel a site fits the bill, I won't promote it. It may be that I only find one site in a year, but that one is likely to be a good one!

The process

First of all, most opportunities will come via a land agent, who manages land for their clients. However, there are also instances where someone may own a house situated within an acre or two, perhaps on the edge of a village, where they wish to try and obtain planning.

Some of the better sites to look at are those on which there is already some form of activity, or where buildings have become redundant – such as commercial use with redundant buildings, because, under the most recent planning guidelines, on sites such as these, you have an incredibly good chance of obtaining planning permission. However, sites for which planning permission may be harder to obtain are those consisting of barren land – especially if that land is in greenbelt. If land is on greenbelt, with no existing buildings, it is extremely tricky indeed to obtain planning permission.

I have viewed sites in the past that initially looked to have great possibilities, only to find out that they were in greenbelt. It can be very disappointing. Remember that, just because land doesn't appear to be 'green and pleasant', does not mean it is not in the greenbelt. Even land that has been used for landfill, but is technically in greenbelt, would be incredibly difficult to get out of greenbelt in order to develop.

Also, ask if the land is in a flood zone as, just because there is no river nearby, or that it doesn't flood, does not mean that it is not. As far as I'm concerned, the rule of thumb is that, if it is in greenbelt then, unless it contains an existing building, it's likely to be too much hassle and a waste of money trying to get planning permission.

Drawing up a promotion agreement

Let's assume you've come across a site where the landowner is prepared to allow you to promote the land on their behalf. The first thing to do is to draw up a Promotion Agreement (your solicitor should be able to do this for you) – ideally, for a five-year term in order for you to have the maximum chance of getting planning permission. The agreement should clearly state that you would receive 30% of whatever price you negotiate with the landowner, should planning be obtained and the land sold. Make sure the agreement states that the land must be sold immediately after planning permission has been granted, otherwise the landowner could hang on to it and you'll never see your money.

Make sure that you also reclaim what you have paid out for obtaining planning permission, prior to receiving 30% of the value of the land. In some cases, the landowner will state a minimum sale price per acre once planning has been obtained. As long as the amount is not too high, this is reasonable, but it is worth taking advice on this from one of the larger agents who specialises in selling sites to house-builders.

The Promotion Agreement also needs to state that you have the ability to appeal any decision against allowing planning permission. In the past, approximately 50% of appeals were upheld and potentially more are now, due to the pressure for new homes, so don't be too despondent should you not get planning permission initially. When you make your planning application, it's always easier to assume that you're likely to have to go to appeal, that way you can make sure that the planning consultant anticipates any issues that the government inspector might have on any particular site.

Obtaining planning consent

So, you've taken advice from your legal team and you have now drafted a watertight, five-year agreement with the landowner. Prior to signing this agreement, you should seek initial planning advice from a planning consultant. There are many planning consultants in the UK today, some of whom will no doubt be local to your area. Do not seek advice from an architect, always from a planning consultant – they are specialists. Ask them about their own experiences and methods, as many of them will have worked with the local authority in the planning department!

Once you have taken initial advice from a planning consultant and you feel there is a reasonable chance that you can get permission from them to put in a pre-application (talked about earlier in this book), the planning authority then have a month in which to come back to you with their advice – at which point, you can decide whether to either proceed further with an outline application, or leave it for now (as you've hopefully got five years). If you feel that there is no chance of being granted planning permission in the future, I would advise contacting the landowner and explaining the situation.

Let's assume that the local authorities are not totally against the idea of granting planning permission. As previously stated, the cost of obtaining outline consent varies greatly, depending on the size of the site you are working on. For a small site, of maybe five units, it will probably cost you in the region of £20,000 to £25,000. However, I have recently been working on a site for 22 houses and I've spent around £50,000 – the bigger the site, the higher the cost.

To summarise, the role of the planning consultant is absolutely essential. They will pull the whole application together for you, advising at every stage as to what expert surveys are required – and knowing the people who can perform them. The planning consultant will also submit the application for you and, should you not be successful, run the planning appeal on your behalf, bringing in any necessary experts. In my experience, you can't work without one.

For an outline planning consent on any site, you're likely to require the following:

- **Topographical survey** – in order to measure the contours of the land.
- **Tree survey** – if there are trees on the site.
- **Ecology survey** – to ascertain whether there are any protected species (such as crested newts) on the site.

- **Layout plan of the site** – showing the properties you will wish to acquire planning on. An architect can draw this up for you, however, this is a simple job as they are not designing the houses at this stage, so make sure they don't make a bigger deal of this than it is.
- **Highways report** – to show that there is a safe visual splay. This means that when you are driving out of the site, you must be able to see in both directions safely and for a reasonable length. If the site entrance is obscured, such as being located on a corner, then you are very likely to have a problem. You need to meet the highways' safety recommendations.
- **Flood risk assessment** – proving that the site is not susceptible to flooding. If it is in a flood zone, you are unlikely to get planning permission.
- **Soil survey** – so you know the soil conditions on the site.
- **Contamination survey** – this will be necessary if it's a brownfield site and has had another use in the past.
- **Historical report** – if there are any listed buildings close by, you will need a report from a historical expert confirming that the new development will not have a detrimental affect on these buildings.

Before you arrange for the surveys above, there are a few extra things that you will need to check: whether there are footpaths on either side of the road, along with street lighting (both good signs); whether there are a school, shop, pub and public transport close by – all of which are big advantages, as they show that the site has sustainability. Also find out whether the site sits within a 30-mile-an-hour zone, along with whether there are houses either side, or next-door.

Bear in mind that, once the application has been submitted and the local authority has had the opportunity to evaluate the site, they are likely to ask for further surveys to be carried out. Unfortunately, this means that, even though you have submitted your application, there may still be added expenses!

If the local authority grants planning permission for less units than you have requested, it is wise to accept their offer, get the planning for those units, and then perhaps look to go back again at a later date if you wish to try and increase the density – some planning is better than no planning!

Dealing with planning issues

Prior to submitting any application to the local authority, I always try to meet with the chairman of the local parish council to show them the plans for my site. I think it shows respect and, even if they are opposed to your initial development, they may suggest an idea that could make your project more acceptable.

If your application does fail, the planning authority will highlight the reason(s) why they have not agreed to your proposal. However, your planning consultant should be able to argue in your favour on appeal, so make sure that you respond to all of the points raised by the planning officer in regards to the reasons why the application failed. Remember, 50% of appeals are usually upheld.

There are two different ways to appeal: you can either submit a written appeal, whereby a single inspector attends the site and submits a report. This is normally the quickest and cheapest, but can still take up to six months; or you can arrange representation, in which case your planning consultant will meet the planning inspectorate and argue the case on your behalf, however, this can take anything up to a year. Some people even go so far as to use a planning barrister for this, but this can mean the costs will escalate significantly. Depending on the reasons as to why the application was refused by the planning authority, I usually opt for a written appeal.

Remember, just because you think a site should get planning, that doesn't mean it will – even if it seems like an obvious conclusion. Always be willing to be flexible, after all, some planning is better than none. Try not to fall out with the planning officer who is dealing with the case – and don't take it personally. And *never* assume you have planning permission until it actually arrives!

Once planning has been granted, there is still a six-week window in which the decision can be challenged by a judicial review. This is not a planning issue, but a legal challenge, such as if it is felt that the application was not dealt with correctly in some way. These legal challenges are becoming more frequent, so be sure that, if you are completing the purchase of land subject to planning, you wait for the six weeks to be over before you complete.

I was recently involved in a deal on a site that had planning turned down by the local authority. We appealed and won, then the local village challenged the decision at a judicial review, which they won! The village believed that it was the end of the matter and celebrated, but we then appealed the judicial review and the decision was overturned – so, in the end, we finally had our planning permission! The planning barrister charged £16,000 a day, but in this case, he definitely earned his money. This was a very unusual matter, however, and the chances of you having to deal with such a complicated planning case are fairly unlikely – so don't worry!

CHAPTER 10:
BACK-TO-BACK DEALS

Back-to-back deals take the ability to trade deals to a completely different level. I have been fortunate enough to be involved in a number of transactions in which I have agreed to purchase a property, then sold it on without actually ever having to pay for it myself – and made a profit in the process.

As an example, I recently agreed to purchase a site, consisting of two existing buildings with planning permission to convert from offices to residential, along with a further site with planning permission for four new houses. I agreed to purchase the whole site for £760,000 and then, through my network of contacts, I managed to find one buyer for the land and one of the office conversions at £550,000, and another buyer wishing to purchase the other office conversion for £325,000. Therefore, the total sales came to £875,000, giving me a profit of £115,000 – for no outlay whatsoever!

Having found the buyers for both elements of the site, I let my solicitor know my intentions and informed my buyers that I was in the process of buying the site myself – implying that I will retain and develop the site should they pull out at any stage.

I then ensured that the person who was selling it to me remained unaware that I was in the process of selling it on, until after I completed the deal. This is extremely important as, even if I end up developing it myself – should my back-to-back transactions fall through – revealing this information would obviously let them know that they have potentially sold it to me for too low a price, or that there is a better way of marketing the site.

Once my solicitor informed me that both my buyers were ready to exchange contracts, I then exchanged with them, while completing my own purchase simultaneously, in a seamless transaction. I used their 10% deposit to exchange contracts on my original purchase.

Stamp duty

One of the issues with the aforementioned type of deal, however, is stamp duty due from the purchaser as this can be over 4%. This is a high cost on the purchase of a property and, if you're not careful, you and your purchaser can both end up paying this, which is a complete waste of money. I usually manage to get the vendor's solicitor to agree that I can assign the contract to another party – meaning that I won't have to pay the stamp duty personally, so only one set of stamp duty is then payable. If they don't agree to this then, unfortunately, the stamp duty will be paid twice – once by myself for the purchase and once by my purchasers for buying it from me.

If you feel you can trust your purchasers, another alternative to both parties having to pay the stamp duty would be to sign an agreement between you both as to how much they will pay you directly, that way they can purchase it straight from the current owner.

The amount then really becomes a form of commission, as they purchase the property directly from the seller. The only problem with this is that there is the risk that the seller and buyer may do the deal directly with each other and cut you out altogether! The best way to avoid this happening is to suggest to the seller that you are involved with the new purchaser.

Over the years I have made £millions through back-to-back deals in this way – some a lot simpler than the example above and some more complicated. My advice overall is to keep the transaction as simple as possible; the more complicated you make it, the more chance there is that it will fail. There is nothing like a back-to-back deal to keep you on your toes!

CHAPTER 11:
WHITE ELEPHANTS

In this instance, a 'white elephant' refers to a building that has become known to have failed in its original form. It could be because it did not sell in the first place, or it was never completed, so becomes notorious for failure. However, if you can find a way of dealing with these problems, then there is an awful lot of money to be made from buildings that no one else wants to purchase.

My first 'white elephant' was a 15-storey tower block in Ipswich, that I purchased along with my backer in 1986. He made sure that I covered all the points I shall be making below before we purchased the 74 flats! I've since gone on to purchase a number of others. The timing of developing these buildings is the key to success, as well as how you deal with any potential issues.

When looking to purchase a property such as this, you need to take extra care when researching the issues you have identified as problems, and then make a judgement call as to whether or not you feel confident that you can overcome these problems – especially if they have haunted the building for many years. If the building has serious structural problems, or has been built in a sub-standard way, these are very good reasons for not buying – some of the best deals are the deals you don't do!

Remember, if buyers have a problem obtaining mortgage approval on your properties once you have completed works, they will not be viable. Even if you are sure that it can be dealt with successfully, always double check with building societies that they agree with your plans, prior to committing to any purchase.

One of the biggest challenges to overcome when purchasing a 'white elephant' is the perception of the general public and any stigma surrounding the building. Nobody wants to be associated with a building that has failed – it's human nature to be drawn to success. Therefore, this is where you will benefit from having an excellent marketing and PR team behind you, to advise you on the best way of re-launching the project. It is also pointless trying to hide the fact that the building has been a problem in the past as, these days, any history can be found with just a quick search on the internet. Confront the issue head on and actively promote the reasons why it is now going to be a success, having eliminated any thought of failure from the project.

As always, we need to look for an 'out' before we have an 'in'. In other words, assess what the worst situation could be should you complete the building but are unable to find buyers. If the upside is huge and the downside is, at worst, minimal, then it may still be worth taking the chance on purchasing the property.

One great thing about 'white elephants' is that they are normally very cheap, either because they have been on the market for a long time and nobody has had the foresight or the nerve to purchase them, or because buyers struggle to borrow money against the property – or a mixture of both. Another advantage is that many developers are wary of making the wrong judgement call and so steer well clear of buildings like these – it's great having no competition when you're buying!

Provided you have prepared yourself for every eventuality, you can then enjoy the ride when you're successful, plus you will also gain a reputation for being a developer who is not afraid to take on difficult projects and will therefore be offered more. And even if your project doesn't bring the results you had hoped, you have already prepared for a worst-case scenario, so you know you can deal with it.

What I find amusing when you are successful with one of these difficult projects is just how many people will claim they were going to buy it before you, or they would have done so if they knew how cheap you got it for! I tend to take these comments with a pinch of salt, after all, 'talk is cheap, it takes money to buy land'.

CHAPTER 12:
THE PERFECT DEAL

Some may say there is no such thing as a perfect deal, just like there is no perfect husband or wife – although whether any husband is brave enough to say so is another matter! – but believe me, in the property world there *are* perfect deals. I'm talking about those deals where there are options regarding what you can do with the property and you can make substantial profits with minimal risk. If a deal has options, it generally means it's a good deal.

When I'm looking to buy, I will always ask myself, "What are my options?" If I only have one – buying, refurbishing and selling it on – it probably means I'll be paying too much for the property. In a case such as this, I have to be totally committed to the refurbishment, the costs involved and the time it will take to complete and sell on. This is likely to be around 18 months. However, if I can purchase the property for the right price, I will probably have four options:

1. The first, most exciting, option is a back-to-back sale. This involves agreeing to purchase a property, but selling it on at a profit to another buyer simultaneously. In effect, you are using your buyer's money to finance the purchase, with no monetary outlay on your part whatsoever. The balance between what they pay you and what you pay

the current owner is instant profit in your bank.

This kind of transaction is also known as flipping – a term I don't personally favour, as it can sometimes be used in the wrong context by those who actually pay for the property themselves and then sell it on at a later date, so not actually a back-to-back deal at all.

When back-to-backing a deal, you really only get one shot at it. It's important to remain aware that it is a risky strategy, especially if you were intending to buy it anyway as, if the original owner discovers your intention, they are highly likely to pull out of the transaction.

2. A second option is to sell the property on, having first completed your purchase, with your new buyer still able to complete a refurbishment and make a decent profit. This buyer will usually have no other option but to refurbish and sell it on.

3. To maximise your return on a deal, a third option is to refurbish it yourself and then put it on the market. This will almost certainly bring the maximum profit, but will probably take around 18 months to complete the sale. Mind you, if you chose to accept a lower profit by choosing options one or two, then there is the added possibility of quickly finding another deal or two to boost the coffers.

4. Your final option is to refurbish a building and then let it. This is a way of refinancing the property and taking profit that way, while still retaining ownership of the building as a long-term investment. Letting a building is a lot quicker and simpler than selling. If I anticipate when a refurbishment will be completed, I can also get the refinancing organised in good time. I'm unlikely to get all the money back that I have invested, but I will certainly receive a healthy percentage – the property will now

be worth a lot more than the purchase price, and the rental income will more than cover my mortgage. I can probably get 75% of my cash back, while still owning the property with equity remaining.

As you can see from the options listed above, if you can purchase a property at a cheap price, there are always a number of options for you as to how you can sell it on for a profit.

I recently had a very good offer on a property that we only bought two months earlier. It would've given us a profit of over £500,000. If we had developed the property we would probably have made a further £800,000. The question my financial backer asked me on this deal was a good one: "If we get our money back, plus £600 000, can we make a further £800,000 easier on another deal, where perhaps we won't need to spend further money developing the property as we would on this one?"

My answer was: "yes, there's always another deal and no one has ever gone bust making a profit!" So my rule, generally, is, if we can sell immediately for at least 40% of the profit we would make by keeping it for two years and developing it, then we sell now.

CHAPTER 13:
TENDERS

A tender is the way that a professional estate agent and/or chartered surveyor brings the marketing of a property to a close at a specific date and time. They may well anticipate that the property will garner huge interest, but are not quite sure what it might go for in the end, so will just give you a price guide and let the market decide.

There are two types of tenders: a formal tender, where, on signing the document, you are legally committing to complete within 28 days; and an informal tender, which is really just about the agent receiving a number of offers at a certain time.

Of these, I only really make offers on informal tenders, because they give you the flexibility to change your mind and renegotiate at a later date, should you think you've made a mistake, or come across any problems after you have done your due diligence.

Informal tenders

If it's an informal tender, you do not commit yourself to any legal agreement. This means that tenders will be opened normally, with the buyer who submits the highest tender then having to prove they have the funds (and, in some cases, the experience) to purchase the property. However, as a buyer, you are not legally committed until you purchase via the usual process through your solicitors and have exchanged contracts. An informal tender is a lot more fun than a formal tender – and a lot less pressure!

In my case, when an agent informs me that they need to receive my offer by 12noon, I will invariably call them at around 12.15pm, apologise for missing the deadline and ask if it is still possible to submit my offer – knowing full well that no agent will risk failing to achieve the best price for their client, by quibbling over 15 minutes. I can then check with the agent and hopefully find out what price I can pay for the property.

In the old days, people would visit the office at the time of which the tender had to be in, sit there waiting to see whether they've been successful or not and witness the opening of the envelopes. These days, this rarely happens, but I still think it was a good way of purchasing a deal.

It's much more difficult to organise the funds for a purchase, if you don't know what it might cost you in the end, so I tend not to worry about the funding of the deal until I know I have been successful. This way, I don't waste my time, other people's time and, most importantly, money doing a lot of investigation work, finding funding and valuations etc., only to be told that I am way off when it comes to the price.

Remember that, with an informal tender, you are under no legal obligation whatsoever to complete the purchase, should things not pan out with the property as you had hoped.

Formal tenders

A formal tender is virtually the same as exchanging contracts in the traditional way, or signing an auction contract – you are legally committed to complete the purchase. The vendor will normally ask you to pay the 10% deposit at the same time as submitting your tender. Provided you are successful and you are deemed to have done all your investigations, you will complete 28 days later.

Always have your funding in order before submitting a formal tender – I've known a number of people who have won formal tenders without doing this, only to find out when they come to complete the deal, that the bank has denied their application. *Never* exchange contracts to purchase any property without knowing you have all your finances in place – it's utter madness and will put you under immense pressure. Even if you have to sell an asset you would have preferred not to sell, or for less than you'd hoped, it is much better to be secure in the knowledge that you have the funds in place to complete.

Be aware that a vendor can sue you if you fail to complete. The first thing you will receive is a legal notice to complete from their solicitors, informing you that you have 14 working days in which to complete the purchase, and that you will be charged interest on the whole sum outstanding. The interest charged will usually be between 4% and 8% over the bank base rate. If you are making a standard purchase, make sure you read this notice carefully before you sign anything. Unfortunately, if you are signing a tender, you will have no chance to do so. If you do think you may be late completing, you can often negotiate this rate down – but there is no point in trying to do this after you have exchanged!

If you fail to complete within the notice period, the vendor can legally keep your 10% deposit and remarket the property. If they end up selling it for less than you had contractually agreed to pay and can prove they've remarketed it in a proper fashion, you will also be liable for the difference.

You'll be pleased to hear, however, that in my experience, very few people get sued for the balance, as the vendor must prove that they have marketed it correctly and have lost out financially — remember, they already have your 10% deposit to add to the sales price they get from the second buyer. Over the years, I've have had a few people unable to complete with me by the agreed date, but I always find it best to work with them and give them more time. This also gives me the opportunity to make more money out of the buyer, because if I give them a further 28 days in which to complete, I'm completely within my rights to add an extra £10,000, £20,000, or even £30,000 to the sale price, to compensate for the inconvenience, stating that otherwise, they will lose their deposit.

I always try to weigh up the bonus of receiving more money, against the chance of the buyer walking away from their 10% deposit — based on the fact that, despite informing a buyer that I will attempt to claim back any loss accrued when the property is re-sold, in reality, they probably know as well as I do that this is incredibly difficult to achieve. The chances are, this will just result in a long-running legal battle between solicitors regarding correct marketing etc., while, in the meantime, the property remains technically sold and you won't have your money.

In an ideal world, it will always be you that is keeping someone else's 10% deposit and not the other way around. Fortunately, I've never been in the situation of not completing, but I am sure it's not a pleasant place to be and, as previously stated, can lead to you having to sell other assets, or borrow money at a high level of interest, in order to complete. Both of which can be avoided if you organise yourself correctly.

Personally, I'm not a great fan of formal tenders, because you're totally committed to purchase. There is no wriggle room whatsoever, so you need to be incredibly confident of what you are doing and that the price you have offered will guarantee you a decent profit. Of course, with a formal tender you may well ultimately reach the same price as an informal tender, due to your financial commitment.

Unless you are already an experienced property purchaser, I would advise you to stick to informal tenders initially. I much prefer them due to the lack of financial commitment and also because you can renegotiate should there be a problem, or something that needs clarification as to whether or not it is part of the deal. The issue with a formal tender, of course, is that you need to make sure you have the funding available to purchase, even without actually knowing whether you're going to get it – which can be costly and frustrating. Although, there is some advantage if you buy at auction, as you can at least see who you are bidding against!

The problem with any tender, whether it is formal or informal, is that you are never aware of the value of other bids. An advantage I have obviously tried to get myself, over others tendering for the same property – never easy, when these tenders have to be submitted by a certain time. Plus, if you ask the agent how much interest there has been in the property and what they think it will go for, they generally wont reveal very much at all. This is to be expected; the fact that the agent is doing this type of sale in the first place tells you that they are professional and are not likely to help you any more than anyone else.

In the past, you could offer to pay £50 higher than the highest offer they receive, however, now the tender documents make it quite clear that your offer has to be a fully declared amount, so you're not really left with much option. On the odd occasion, I have contacted an agent after the tender deadline, informing them that I have accidentally missed the closing time and asking if it still possible to put an offer in – and, if so, at what figure. Because the agent's job is to get the highest purchase price for their client, this can often be a successful trick. I doubt the agent's client would be best pleased if they found out you were prepared to pay substantially more than the best tender so, in my experience, in such instances the agent will nearly always be helpful.

Another trick is to deliberately make a mistake on the tender form, so that you can make contact with the agent and talk through the problem. For example, you could put an extra zero on the informal tender, meaning it will be obvious that it is a mistake and the agent will have to ring you and find out what your true offer is.

In the past, buyers would sometimes just sit in an agent's office until the time of the tender, see who else walked in with tenders and then decide what to offer on the basis of who had come into the office. They obviously had more time on their hands back in those days!

CHAPTER 14:
DEALING WITH THE LARGER BUILDER AND CONTRACTOR

It's an interesting observation that, once a building company grows beyond a certain size, rather than being referred to as builders, they will prefer to be known as contractors. Many years ago, my first backer advised me to never choose a builder who is financially bigger than you – in other words, make sure you always have the financial upper hand. If your builder is financially stronger and you find yourselves in a dispute, they are in a far stronger position to hold out and get their own way, or to take you to court. Remember, until any dispute is resolved, there is a possibility that no properties may be sold on the completed project, which will create added pressure for you and, of course, they will know that.

Costs

When I'm looking to appoint a builder on a development, I make sure that the value of the contract is never more than a third of their annual turnover, in other words, if the contract price is £2m, I want them to have a turnover of at least £6m per annum.
The reason for this is that, if they make a mistake pricing my contract, they should hopefully still have enough cash flow and

profit from their other contracts not to go bankrupt, or need to come back and try to re-negotiate the original contract price.

I will also be concerned if the builder currently has a large amount of ongoing work, yet still wishes to take on more. However good their organisation is, if they overstretch themselves work-wise, they will land themselves – and you – with big problems.

It is common sense to also choose a builder who is based relatively close to your site. If they are located 200 miles away, then they are likely to find it difficult to manage the site and all that comes with it.

Large or small?

When deciding on who will do the works on your site, if it is a small contractor and this will be the only project they will have on, it's very tempting to appoint them – the thinking being that they will be able to give your project their full attention. However, I recommend you do some research as to why they have no other current work. It's also very unlikely they will have the cash flow to do a proper month's work, prior to receiving your payment for their first month's valuation of works carried out. If they do complete the initial month, you also need to double check that they are not over-valuing the work they have done in order to help their cash flow.

Incentive

During my many years in the property business, I have looked at the best and cheapest ways of developing projects. For instance, I've purchased all the materials myself and so am only charged for the labour. I have also employed everybody myself too. The trouble with both of these options is that there is is little or no incentive for the contractor to get the work completed quickly.

Another way that contractors often like to work is 'Cost Plus'. Basically, this is open-book accounting, the idea being that the client is shown all costs and then an agreed percentage is added. Again, with this system, I see no incentive for the contractor to get the job done on time, or on budget, as they are in a win-win situation.

I therefore think it is essential that the contractors have some skin in the game; that there is an incentive for them to perform and financial penalties if they fail. After all, a job that overruns and costs more will certainly affect the developer enormously in terms of interest payments to the bank, cash flow and their ability to buy the next deal.

Contracts

At this point I have to say that I have awarded literally hundreds of millions of pounds worth of building work to numerous companies and individuals over the years, and have never had a contract come in both on time and on budget. It is often just one or the other, or sometimes neither. For some projects, this is simply down to the nature of the works – converting buildings is notoriously difficult to estimate and, therefore, there is almost always extra work needed during construction. New builds, as discussed in an earlier chapter, are considerably easier.

Bearing all the above in mind, I am convinced – as are the banks, without whose support most developments are highly unlikely to proceed – that the only way to deal with any builder/contractor is by way of a Fixed Price Contract. First up, a Full Schedule of Works needs to be prepared. Make sure this is incredibly thorough because, the larger the contractor you use, the more adept they will be at finding any loopholes or mistakes, for which they can add extra charges. Of course, as they are already on site, no other company will be allowed to carry out additional work and they really hold all the cards.

Remember, once you have signed the Building Contract, they are technically in control of the site until it is handed back to you on completion of the work.

Tradesmen and contractors

In the past, big companies would employ all tradesmen in-house, such as plumbers, electricians, carpenters and so on. That has all changed. Nowadays, these companies are highly skilled management organisations, who sub-contract out all the work, add a percentage on top of what they get charged, and pass this on to the client. This is normally in the region of 10% to 15%. I have recently awarded a £25m contract to a contractor who only has 20 direct workforce employees on site at any one time, out of a total workforce of around 200.

As a client, you will most likely never see the sub-contractor prices. On top of this, there are also preliminary costs that you will be expected to cover, namely their set-up costs to be on site. This includes things such as site office, restroom, all the insurances they require, hire of equipment etc. – the list is endless and I have to admit that it drives me mad! There aren't many businesses where you get paid all your costs separately, on top of your profit!

To justify these costs, a contractor will argue that they are taking all the risk, to which I, grudgingly, have to agree. If a sub-contractor goes bust halfway through the project, then clearly the contractor has the problem, rather than you. There will be a clause in your Building Contract that allows you to claim against the contractor financially, should they not complete the project on time. This financial penalty will have been agreed with the contractor before the job commenced and the amount stated clearly on the Building Contract. It should be enough to make it hurt should they fail.

I must point out that, should they not finish the project on time, most contractors are likely to come up with every excuse under the sun as to why this was the case – even down to the weather conditions! And, annoyingly, most of which they will claim is your fault! Unfortunately, late completion is common and something you have to learn to deal with.

But what do you do if they do more than just finish late? Unfortunately, however experienced you are, there will still be some builders and contractors who make financial mistakes with projects that bring them down.

Depending on how big a disaster it is and how far into the project they are, my general advice is to support them as best you can, in order that they can finish your job. They are still likely to be cheaper than to trying to get in another company – who, knowing the situation, are likely to take advantage of this. A new company will also be unfamiliar with the site and will need extra time to get up to speed.

When things go wrong, there is also the risk that the original contractor may not have been paying their sub-contractors. This is a real problem, because the last thing you want is for workers to arrive at the site and start ripping out work that has already been done, because they have not been paid for it!

There are a couple of tell-tale signs to look out for as an indication as to whether or not a contractor is struggling with cash flow, or the enormity of the project:

Firstly, they will be behind schedule and making excuses as to why – things like the bathrooms have not been delivered on time, or the windows came but were not the right size so they had to be sent back. Secondly, there won't be many people on site – I never let contractors know when I am visiting, that way I get a much better idea of how things are really going! Eventually, of course, they will usually own up and reveal all the problems, but not before a lot of time and effort has been wasted – which is totally unacceptable.

If I have the smallest concern about a contractor, I will contact the sub-contractors first to find out whether they have been paid. There is nothing that annoys and frustrates me more than paying the main contractor for work that has been done, only for them not to pass that money on to the sub-contractor who has actually done that work. Initially, sub-contractors may remain loyal to the main contractor, as they may well give them lots of work, however, it is still worth leaving your number with them – they will soon be back in touch when they haven't been paid! If this does end up being the case, you can then agree to pay your sub-contractors directly, and deduct this money from the total sum of the main contractor's contract – at least that way they will still turn up!

CHAPTER 15:
DOING BIGGER
AND BIGGER DEALS

As you progress through your property-developing career, increasingly, you will be doing bigger deals (unless you make a conscious decision that you want to remain at a certain level).

In many ways the big deals are easier, because you are more likely to rely on professional consultants, who have the ability and experience to deliver the completed project. Any bank or funder you use will require you to have these experts in place, to ensure that the development is successful.

It may well be that you need a number of consultants for your project. It could be that you require a quantity surveyor, a structural engineer and an architect, as well as a cost consultant and acoustic engineers etc. Luckily, these days you can often locate all the necessary experts within one practice – I find this easier than going to individual consultants, which is much more time consuming.

What you have to appreciate about all these consultants is that they are often dealing with even bigger projects than yours, so may not be used to being challenged on every decision and price they come up with. Quite often, they are acting on behalf of a government organisation, or consulting on the build of a new school building. If they have private clients, they are generally not property developers; it is far more likely for them to be private buyers, who want a building built for their own occupation.

Many have ambitions to do bigger and bigger deals as everybody thinks that the bigger the deal you do, the more profit you make – I can assure you that is not always the case. Very few of my bigger deals have been as profitable pro rata as my smaller ones and the risks involved in doing them have been much, much greater.

Obviously, the potential of the big deal is very enticing, not just the profit you can make, but also quite often the publicity and the admiration that goes with it. However, you really have to put any ego to one side and remember, if it goes wrong, the publicity will be far worse for you than any publicity would've been if it went right – and could set you way back in your career.

I look at this kind of situation a bit like a game of 'snakes and ladders'; you start off doing small deals, getting more and more confident and you end up three quarters of the way up the ladder. Then you make one slip, lose a lot of money and end up right back down at the bottom doing the small deals again

Over the years, I have been quite unique amongst the bigger developers, in as much as that I still enjoy doing the very small deals – it keeps me very grounded and the profits normally come much quicker. So, I'm not saying don't try and do bigger deals. because that is ambition and we all really want to do that, but do be extra careful, because one big deal that goes wrong could bring you down, whereas just one out of five or six smaller deals probably won't.

Making your first million

When I began doing deals back in the 1980s, £1m was worth a lot more than it is today, however, I can tell you that it still feels fantastic when you've made £1m on any deal.

I am fortunate enough to have made £1m profit for myself and my partners on a number of occasions, however, I have to say that, by the time I've actually completed on the deal, I'm usually mentally drained and exhausted. However, I quite often just move on, reinvesting the whole amount into the next project, so never really have the time to appreciate or enjoy our success. There is a well-known phrase: 'you're only as good as your next deal', and there will always be those in the property world who will have more money, make more money and become even more successful than I have been – I'm hoping that, after reading this book, you may well become one of them. If you do, please do give me a mention sometime in the future!

It is often said that making money is hard and keeping hold of it is even harder and this is something I would totally agree with. There will always be those who will want to know you if they think you are successful. They will offer you deals that they can't fund themselves, however, there is usually a good reason why this is the case; typically, it's because they don't have the skill or experience! These people are always looking to find someone who will fall for their patter – make sure it's not you!

Whether or not to take the risk

Everybody makes mistakes in the property world; so don't be disheartened if you get it wrong sometimes. The trick is to make sure the losses are few and far between.

Booker T Washington once said, "associate yourself with people of good quality, for it is better to be alone than in bad company". I've always made a conscious effort to surround myself with the most honest, decent people I can and also, as you generally get what you pay for, try to pay as much as I can afford for my advisors – and take their advice! They are likely to be brighter than I am, even if maybe not as bold!

Of course, as you get older – and hopefully wiser – it is almost certain that you will become more cautious and take fewer risks. One of the reasons for this could be that you don't want to lose what you have gained up to that point, plus you could also now have the responsibility of a spouse and family. You may have met people who have lost everything and worry that the same thing could happen to you, but generally these people are those who have become reckless; those who let a little success go to their head and take bigger risks with each deal, mistakenly believing everything they touch will turn to gold.

Always be aware of the consequences of any decisions you make. When you first start out, having only a little knowledge can sometimes make you overly brave, because you don't know any better. Of course, now and again the deals will come off, which can give you a false sense of security, but this is dangerous ground. Hopefully this book will help you avoid making such mistakes.

If things do go wrong, remember, it doesn't mean your next deal will also be a disaster. Always believe in yourself and the experience you have gained, and get back in the running. With a little more caution, you will do a better deal next time – there is nothing wrong with being a prudent property developer.

Obviously, big risks are not for everybody – all risks are relative to the person who is taking them – and you may not always make the millions that you'd hoped for, but as your career progresses, with diligence and experience, you will be able to sleep at night, put food on the table and hopefully have the quality of life you are looking for.

CHAPTER 16:
DEALING WITH
OTHER DEALERS

Inevitably, once you start doing a number of deals, you will probably be dealing with people like yourself – dealers who understand the business and that everyone has to make a profit. When I first started out in this business, I was taught to always leave something for somebody else; never leave a fellow dealer with no option but to come back to you at the end and have to ask for the price to be reduced. Try to build a rapport with like-minded people, that way the chances of this happening become very slim.

When you're buying from another dealer, try not to concern yourself with how much money they are making from the deal. If you are completely confident in your own ability, then whether they are making a large profit, or very little should be of no concern to you.

When I'm giving one of my speeches, I often tell the story of how, in 1991, we purchased two tower blocks in West Bromwich, Sandwell, each consisting of 140 flats. The Irish property dealer paid £75,000 for each block six months earlier, so a total of £150,000. We paid him £1.5m for them! We got to the point where we were ready to exchange, but his solicitor couldn't get hold of him, so I called his home and his wife said he'd gone to an antiques fair at Stafford Showground. I jumped in my car and drove for three and a half hours, found him on his stall selling bric-a-brac and asked him if we are still doing the deal, to which he said he wanted more money. I told him I would pay another £50,000, but he had to ring his solicitor there and then, using my phone, and instruct him to exchange – which he did!

Nobody wants to pay more than they have to, however, I have always admired his tenacity. At the time, we were probably the only buyer for such a deal, so to risk it for £50,000 was very brave of him. I was very confident that I could make a lot of money out of the blocks, so it didn't concern me that he had probably just sealed the deal of his lifetime!

Great character

When I first started in this industry, there seemed to be a lot more characters about than there are today; these people often had great charisma and could buy and sell – not just property, but also anything else they put their mind to.

They are great fun to be around, great company and make for a great night out. Everybody wants to know them and they seem to just flow through life without any issues or problems, making money with ease.

The truth is, however, that they probably have just as many problems as the rest of us, but either don't worry about it, or are great at putting on a brave face. Everyone has bad days in property, the trick is not to have too many of them.

A word of caution, however, if you do come across characters like this, enjoy their company, but if they say to you "do you know what, I've got just the deal for you", take a step back and let someone else take the rollercoaster ride – not you!

CHAPTER 17:
COMMERCIAL INVESTMENTS AND DEVELOPMENT

Large commercial development

Large commercial development is clearly very important; without it, we wouldn't have any shops to shop in, restaurants to eat in, warehouses to deliver our online orders, supermarkets in which to buy our food or, dare I say it, government departments from which to try and run the country, to name just a few. Commercial developers clearly hold a very important place within our society and in the running of the country – something you may not have considered before you started reading this book.

I've always considered commercial development less risky than residential development and also that the people who deal in this market are more risk-adverse than those who specialise in residential. The reason being that virtually no commercial developers build anything on spec, which means that they will only build a commercial unit once they have a tenant signed up in a pre-let agreement, or have agreed to sell it in a pre-sale agreement.

Of course, some of these commercial developments are extremely large. When developing a new shopping centre, or out-of-town retail or distribution warehousing, it would take a brave person to do so without having any end users committed to occupying the completed development.

Most commercial developers buy land subject to planning permission. This reduces the risk right at the start. At the same time, they will appoint a commercial agent to seek out suitable tenants to occupy the units when they are completed. Ideally, the agent will have ample time in which to sign up these tenants, before the developers are fully committed to purchasing the site.

Once tenants have been sourced, the development is fully covered. Planning is obtained, all tenants will have signed an Agreement to Lease, and the developers will have put the job out to tender, so as to receive fixed-price building quotes to build out the development from a selection of building contractors. What can possibly go wrong?

Well, fortunately, the answer is generally not a lot, although, of course, some contractors have been known to go bankrupt over the years, and other unexpected problems can sometimes occur. Recently, I heard of a developer who brought in a company to set out his site ready to build, however, only when the buildings were almost completed, did the contractor realise that that they weren't in the correct position! All the buildings had to be taken down and rebuilt in their correct position, as per the original planning permission! Luckily, my friend was fully insured, otherwise this could have been a very costly mistake .

With a large development, most developers will want to get one big tenant signed up first. These are called anchor tenants, the idea being that securing a big name will then attract other tenants, in the confidence that they can trade from there, knowing that there will be a lot of foot traffic going to the anchor tenant.

Funding new commercial developments

As explained in the previous chapter, because most large commercial developments are pre-let – either partly or fully – it often makes the funding of such projects a lot easier than with residential. This is because the bank or institution lending on the project can see that rental income will be coming in from the day the project is completed.

In fact, many developers actually pre-sell a whole scheme subject to the completion of the building works and the tenants moving in. This can be a seamless transaction from start to finish; for example, purchasing the site subject to planning in the first place, then finding tenants prior to committing to the purchase of the land, then at that point, finding an institutional-type buyer – such as an insurance company – to purchase the project from them on completion.

As all the tenants are signed up prior to the work commencing, some of these institutional buyers will also fund the build costs for the developer, before completing the purchase once the project is completed and the tenants have moved in.

These days, a number of local authorities are also getting in on the act as they are now allowed to purchase investment properties, not just within their local area, but across the whole of the UK – a concession that has caused some controversy. People can understand a local authority investing in their own area, but not in other local authoritys' areas, which some have done. Of course it's the rate payers' money they're probably investing, but they also have the ability to borrow money at very cheap interest rates – unlike the rest of us!

Some developers don't want to sell the investment on once it's completed, but instead wish to retain it as a future long-term investment. Funding these investments is often made a lot easier because the tenants are national covenants. Tenants who are public limited companies, or have multiple outlets across the country, are also more likely to sign up for a minimum of 10 years, giving you extra security. A good set of accounts is also essential – remember, even large companies can go bankrupt. They may well also fit out their own units, which also adds to their commitment to staying long-term. In such cases, most banks will lend on a long-term basis to the developer – usually, the length of the leases to the tenants will mirror the length of the loan from the bank. I call a deal like this, where it is basically self-funding, the perfect commercial deal! Although a lot of work and experience might be required, along with a bit of luck, ultimately this kind of deal poses no risk whatsoever to the developer.

Commercial values and tenants

The way that you value let commercial property is by way of the percentage yield you receive, in other words, the rent. The shorter the lease and the weaker the tenant – in terms of financial ability to pay – dictates the yield. For instance, if the lease only has five years left to run to a local covenant (i.e. a local business), the yield might be 10% of the freehold value, meaning that, if the rent is £10,000 per annum, the property should sell for £100,000. If you have a larger company – such as Boots the Chemist, for example – as a tenant on a new 10-year lease, at a rent of £10,000 per annum, then the yield might be 5%, which would value the property at £200,000. These are two very simple examples and, as you can see, the longer the lease to a strong covenant such as a national company, the more the building is worth, while with the shorter lease let to a local business, the value is less.

Of course, there are many variations, usually based on the length of the lease, the tenant, or whether the building is worth more vacant and can be developed for another type of use than the current one.

Nearly all the commercial leases in the UK have upward-only rent reviews, which means that, at the very worst, on a rent review which normally takes place after three or five years, the rent stays the same. Interestingly, this was the same in Ireland right up until the property recession of 2008, after which, the Irish Government changed the law, so that rents could go down as well as up at this review. This had a huge knock-on effect on the value of commercial property in certain areas of Ireland, as some rents went down by as much as half, because landlords had no rental evidence to substantiate the rent they were asking for. In some cases, the shops surrounding the shop due for a rent review had become vacant, or re-let at half the cost of what they had been rented for previously.

Most leases will state that a property must be left, on vacation, in the same condition as when it was initially rented by the tenant. This is normally ensured by collecting photographic evidence as well as, in most cases, a Schedule of Condition – provided by a chartered surveyor, prior to the tenant taking possession.

If, when vacated, the property is not in the same condition, a schedule of works is prepared by a chartered surveyor. The tenant will often dispute this, however, so a negotiation takes place. A financial settlement is usually agreed and the tenant does not carry out the works required, but leaves it for the landlord to arrange after the financial reimbursement has been received. Of course, they could opt to repair the building themselves if they so wish.

If you are buying an investment property, it's well worth making sure that there is a Schedule of Condition included within the lease, because, in most cases, it is a bonus for the landlord to obtain a cash settlement from the tenant at the end of the lease, should there be any works needed. After all, you may well be able to rent it to the next tenant in its current condition and not have to spend any money refurbishing it after all. Sometimes, an alternative option is to give the ingoing tenant a three-month rent-free period to do such works themselves.

It is also wise to remember that, at the end of any lease, as the landlord, you will be responsible for paying the empty rates until the building is re-let – unless the property is a listed building, in which case, there will be no costs to pay.

It is essential to always do a financial check on all the tenants that are in the building, prior to your purchase. An agent may make a big song and dance about a tenant who has numerous branches nationally and a massive turnover, but there's no guarantee that you won't find out later that they lost £100million the year before and are highly unlikely to be in business a year later – unfortunately, a scenario I have experienced myself!

When you are buying a commercial investment at auction, or subject to contract, you must make sure that there is not a clause in the contract stating that you have to pay all the arrears of the existing tenant. This is quite common, especially in auction contracts, and it is very easy to be caught out,. Make sure you have checked that you're not having to take on this responsibility and will have to try to claim it back off the tenant at a future date. There is clearly a good reason why they haven't or won't pay!

You also need to make sure that the rents coming in are as watertight as possible, and will continue to come in once you have purchased the investment. If they are local tenants, with, say, just one shop or two, check that, within the lease, they have signed a personal guarantee on the rent. This means that, if the business fails, they are personally liable to pay the rent themselves as owners of the business. Also, make sure that all the rents are up to date, everyone has paid and that there is no rent outstanding.

If, after having purchased the investment, a tenant does find themselves in financial difficulty, I always try and work it through with them, rather than insisting they pay the three months in advance, which is probably what your lease will say. I will, instead, usually allow them to pay monthly to help with their cash flow – in fact, I will do as much as I can to keep them in the property. Remember, if they go bankrupt and the property ends up being vacant for a length of time, it will be you paying the empty rates – a fact that does tend to concentrate the mind somewhat, as these can be very expensive. Also, you may find that current rent values have dropped, and you can no longer achieve the rent that you did with the original tenant.

If I have a vacant shop and I have a potential tenant approach me, who hasn't been in business before, I will do my best to help, support and advise them along the way. Ultimately, you won't receive any rent if their business fails, so this is a sensible approach to take and one that has stood me in good stead over the years.

Developing secondary commercial investments

When I'm looking at secondary shop investment – in other words, those that may be in a poorer part of the town centre, or on the outskirts of the town – I concentrate on the ones that normally have vacant upper floors. This provides me with the opportunity to convert into residential flats. If they are currently vacant, or let at a very low rent, it usually means that, on the overall price you pay for the property, it will give you an opportunity to make money.

Conversion of these spaces has been made a lot easier over the last few years by the Government's change to the planning law, which now allows what is known as 'permitted rights'. This means that, if the property has been used as offices within the past three years, then you can submit a proposal to your local planning department, stating how many flats you wish to create within the building conversion. The planning department then have four weeks in which to accept your proposal and issue you with a certificate. You will also require building regulation approval, – once you have this, you may then start the development.

If you wish to change any of the external look of the

building, you may well require full planning permission. This could trigger payments for social housing and a community infrastructure levy charge, which you will usually have to pay under normal planning permission, so please check with the authority before making any such changes. However, if no external changes are planned, these costs will not be incurred and there is a great opportunity to make a good profit out of such a development

The area in which you are developing, alongside what the shops below your planned conversion are currently used for, play a big part in whether or not you should purchase and develop the property. If there are restaurants below the property, you may find that the buyers will struggle to get a mortgage because they are above such businesses and their inherent noises or smells. In which case, I would strongly advise you not to purchase such a property.

So, assuming the property was suitable, and having developed the upstairs to sell off – or possibly rent out – I will then try to increase the value of the ground floor shops by renegotiating with the existing tenants, in the hope that they will sign longer leases, which should put up the value of the property when I decide to sell it.

Please note that, although it is tempting to sell on the shop part of an investment prior to completing the residential upper floors as it will be great for cash flow, personally, I normally resist this. This is because, if there are any problems and I need to gain access to the shops below for building work, it is far easier to do so if I am still the landlord, rather than having to approach another owner, who may not be as accommodating.

I might also struggle to sell the flats individually, in which case, I will still have the flexibility of letting the flats out and selling the whole building as an investment property.

It may well be that you discover an entire building that is vacant, including the shops below. In such a case, it is wise to ask yourself why this is the case, although, having said this, a common answer tends to be that there is much less of a need for physical shops these days, due to online shopping.

Unfortunately, in some areas of the country the local planning departments don't always agree with your ideas, so although you may think the building could be converted completely into flats, or even houses, or knocked down, be very careful – local authorities often do not like losing buildings that can create employment, not to mention business rates. However, if you do some research, you may find that planning is being obtained nearby that will transform the area, so shops will once more be required, or, if they are currently partly let, they will be in demand again.

A word of caution: a few years ago, there was a new shopping centre planned in Ipswich, so I purchased a row of shops close by, foreseeing that my shop rents would double due to the close proximity of the new centre. What I failed to appreciate was that my shops were facing the rear of the new centre, not the front, meaning that the rents of my shops hardly increased at all!

Funding secondary commercial property

This refers to mortgaging and re-mortgaging secondary commercial investment properties – sometimes difficult to finance.

One of the biggest problems is that some banks are very nervous about lending on this type of investment, where some tenants have not been in business long and are small local businesses. These tenants often only like to sign a fairly short lease term – sometimes between (as low as) one and five years – and even then, some like to include a break clause within that period (normally three years), meaning that the rent is only guaranteed for three years as they may not wish to remain for the other two. Understandably, this means that banks will be particularly cautious, unless there are a large number of different tenants in the one parade of shops, in which case, the risk is spread and minimal.

But all is not lost; there are now banks that specialise in lending on this type of secondary shop investment. However, they are expensive and you may well find that they will charge a high interest rate, which, in turn, reduces the amount of capital they will lend you. In other words, if the rent coming in per month is £5,000, they probably would not want the repayments to them to be more than £2,500 per month, which is 100% cover on the rent coming in. This is because the banks consider tenants who rent secondary shop premises to be more of a risk than larger regional and national businesses. Clearly, this restricts the amount of money you can borrow over a period of time.

Having said that, there are ways that you can increase your borrowing potential. If you can increase your rental income, then you can have the investment re-valued and, if the property has a higher value, you will be able to borrow more. You could also sell off part of the investment if there are a number of self-contained shops. Quite often, the smaller the investment in terms of value, then the more small investors it should appeal to. You can then use that money to reduce your current mortgage and re-finance. It may be that you could also sell off the upper parts of the property on a new 125-year lease, or similar. However, I would not advise you to sell the freehold as you would be retaining the shops below the upper accommodation, and when you sell the rest of your investment, it will sell much better freehold than it will on a long lease.

Other commercial investments

Commercial investment covers a large range of investments. We have already visited big commercial developments and the secondary shop investment market, so now let's take a look at some other options.

Anything that is not residential is classed as commercial, but that is not saying that you should be investing in all of them. Personally, I have a rule that I find very useful: if it's a poorly let investment – in other words, if it is let to a weak tenant with no financial history behind them, or in poor condition, or on a short lease, or all three – then, unless I have a plan to convert it to residential in some way, however good the short term rent is, I don't buy it.

There are, of course, exceptions to every rule. I know those who specialise in buying lock-up garages all across the UK. They own thousands of them, bringing in great income, and many of the garage blocks they have purchased have now been granted residential planning permission.

Many years ago, one of the most famous alternative forms of commercial investment was in NCP car parks. What a fantastic business it is and, over the years, similar companies have copied their lead. Now, of course, many of their car parks have been successfully developed.

The rule of thumb is that, if it's a slightly obscure investment, then the yield probably needs to be between 10% and 15% – especially if it's on a short lease.

Remember that, unlike more traditional shop investments, a good many of these properties are worth more if they are vacant, providing you can obtain planning permission for an alternative to their existing use.

Where residential and commercial can meet is within the office market, where a property currently let for offices could be worth a great deal more after being developed into residential flats. The problem then is not the rental income you are receiving, but how to obtain vacant possession.

I've overseen many of these projects over the years, as

well as converting hotels, maltings buildings and workhouses –
transforming properties that were originally built for commercial
purposes into residential living spaces.

CHAPTER 18:
BUYING FROM
LARGER COMPANIES

Over the years, I have had great success in purchasing properties from larger companies. One of the reasons for this is that they are often selling a building which was probably purchased to run as a business, not as a development project. They may have owned it for many years, but now no longer require it, and as it's probably had its value written down in their accounts, they are able to sell it on reasonably priced for a quick sale.

Because of the size and wealth of the company, the board of directors are likely to take the view that to get it off the books and get some money back is an advantage.

Recently, I purchased a property from Adnams Brewery, based in Southwold. They were very keen to exchange and have the sale completed prior to publication of their half-year results – something worth taking into account if you purchase from a public company. I am also currently purchasing a building from Marks & Spencer – one which has already been to auction and remained unsold. I have offered them 65% of the auction reserve price, and they have agreed the sale. I am confident that the amount I am paying them pro rata is fairly insignificant and that it is the fact that the property will be off their books, meaning they will no longer be paying empty rates on the building, that is the defining factor in the transaction.

There are also deals you can make with larger property developers and builders who may have inherited a small site having purchased a bigger portfolio. They will often regard these small schemes as just not worth their while developing and will happily sell them on. Similar to the M&S scenario, I recently purchased some land from a major house builder for £220,000 after it failed to sell at auction at a reserve price of £325,000. The land did not have planning permission, so I was taking a calculated risk that I would be able to obtain this, however, the pre-application advice from the Planning Department was that a commercial building with flats above would be acceptable on the site.

Although it took a year to obtain planning permission, I eventually tripled my investment, selling it for £625,000. A prime example of how you can take advantage of the situation when a large company has no inclination to get planning themselves and sell on – what's the saying, "...crumbs from a rich man's table."?

I have also purchased a commercial building, with potential for residential above. I believe that, by using my planning expertise and improving and managing the shops better, I can turn it (in other words, sell it on with planning permission) for around 50% more than I paid, within six months.

It's all about working harder and smarter than the big boys, who may well have no one in their ranks that has ever actually done a property deal of their own. After reading this book, there is a good chance you will become more knowledgeable within the industry than the average member of these large companies, firstly, because they may well be too arrogant to have even read this book, and secondly, because you'll be making deals (if you're not already) – something most never have the courage to do!

Robert Boyce, my first backer, always told me not to be intimidated by someone who works for a big company; it doesn't mean they are better than you, in fact, it probably means they are not!

CHAPTER 19:
MAKING BIGGER DEALS AFTER AUCTION

I have said *after* auction because, if you want to buy the property *before* the auction, it is usually likely to cost you more than the reserve price, unless there has been absolutely no interest. It is often very difficult for the auctioneer to persuade a vendor to sell prior to an auction, because the seller will always hope for lots of interest in their property on auction day. Most auctioneers also want to have as many properties in the room to sell, so will not be keen to go down this route in the first place, whether it's the right advice or not to the client.

If you buy a property in an auction room, you will be paying at least the reserve. At the actual auction, you're not going to get it for less and, if the auctioneer is very good, you may end up paying a lot more than the reserve figure, even if you were the only bidder.

Remember, the idea is to buy the property for as much under the market price as you can, which probably means below the reserve price – and sometimes well below. The only way you're really going to do this – if the property is unsold – is by waiting until after the auction and making an offer. On occasions, however, this may mean quite a while afterwards, as immediately after the auction, you may find that the vendor of the property is still in denial of the outcome, and is questioning their advisers as to why it has not sold at the price that they had recommended. However, this is not your problem – your priority is to buy well under the reserve price and make yourself a lot of money.

It is a lot easier to achieve this when you are buying larger properties, especially commercial ones. These are much more likely to be owned by a commercial company, rather than a private individual, and one who may well just see the property as surplus to their requirements. Agreeing to sell it for what you consider a cheap price doesn't really hurt anybody, financially or personally, except maybe some unsuspecting shareholders – the evidence of which can probably be lost within the annual accounts somewhere!

As previously mentioned, when dealing with these bigger companies, it is very possible to pay just 60% to 70% of the reserve price after the auction. Do not be bullied by the auctioneer, or feel embarrassed by offering this sort of discount, any offer has to be reported to the client and, quite often, the vendor will accept this type of reduction, whatever the auctioneers may say. Remember, if the property is not sold, the auctioneer receives no commission. In the auctioneer's contract with the seller, it usually states that the seller is under contract to pay the auctioneer commission for up to a month after the auction. No seller likes to pay two lots of commission, so it's unlikely that the property will be sold by another firm during this time.

If the vendor doesn't agree to sell the property to you for the sum you have offered, don't despair, be patient. Once the auctioneer's contractual month is up, you will need to track who is selling the property and keep in touch with the new agent. Start up a relationship with this agent and make sure you ask that they let you know should someone else be interested in the property. At this point, however, there is little point in making an offer; it is best to wait until it has been on the market for a couple of months and the new agent has exhausted his contacts and marketing. Then it's fun time – fill your boots and make your deal of the year, or even a lifetime!

I've achieved this myself on many occasions. The thing to remember is that, if after auction, their property has not sold, the seller is often out of options. The chances are that it has already been for sale on the open market and no doubt has also had the asking price reduced to go into the auction, so if the property still fails to sell, you are clearly the buyer of last resort – a compliment in my world!

CHAPTER 20:
DEALING WITH PROFESSIONAL CONSULTANTS

The great thing about doing small deals is that you can often do all the work yourself and not need to rely on other people – something I still enjoy very much.

However, when you begin doing bigger deals, you need to have a top team of consultants on your side. Aside from the fact that it's good practice, the bank you wish to borrow the money from will expect it. If you choose not to use consultants, your bank is likely to have very little confidence in what you do and, worse still, is unlikely to lend you the money.

Part of my success has always been to surround myself with the very best people I can find, in the hope that they are more knowledgeable than I am (which in many cases, is not difficult.)

Most consultants will not undertake doing a deal themselves, but are great at advising others to do so. This is partly because the nature of the beast is one of caution and professionalism, and consultants are generally not risk takers.

Another reason being that they don't *need* to take any risks, because you will be paying them a lot of money for their expertise and experience, in order to safeguard your development and ensure it is a great success.

As you are the one paying them, however, one thing to always remember is to make sure they don't end up just telling you what you want to hear. Treat them with the respect they deserve and make sure they are not so weak as to be able to be bullied by you mentally – because you are stronger than them and also as they are working for you.

For this reason, you need to find the best consultants you can, so these issues do not come up. I need to be told by the people who advise me what the score really is. I certainly don't want some weak-willed, naive consultant preventing me from taking on a development because they give me feeble advice. If you think this might be the case, seek a further opinion.

I need to respect and value my consultants' advice and they need to respect me for my ability, however, it is their job to ensure that I don't get into any dangerous situation that risks my money, my financial backers' money, or that of the bank.

When you have established dealing with a partner, be mindful, as some consultants may then put you in touch with someone who has just recently qualified. I resist this at all costs. Not because I don't like to see young people getting on, but because I'm paying for a top person, and it is pretty much guaranteed that you will not receive a discount if you are merely dealing with one of their assistants. Unless they are exceptional, it will slow the project down, and I certainly don't want to be the client they are using to learn and make mistakes with. Let them use another client for that.

Also be aware of the very large consultancy firms, who often have international offices. They will rarely act for single individuals, but instead for large companies and governments. These types of consultants are no good for your business whatsoever, as will not understand or have the necessary experience to deal with smaller clients – and, on top of this, will be incredibly expensive!

I have to admit, I do resent paying consultants the large sums of money that are required on a bigger development. I'm currently in the process of paying one consultancy firm in excess of £450,000, which, as you can imagine, breaks my heart – especially as, on this occasion, I really don't feel that they are worth it! However, as a great friend of mine pointed out, without using them, I could not proceed with the development in the first place – and of course, the consultants know this.

So choose your consultants wisely. Get advice from other developers who have used them, make sure they're not going to be holding back any development you wish to do, trust them, respect them and pay them well.

Good consultants will not only make you a lot of money, they will also prevent you from losing a lot of money – and potentially even stop you from going bankrupt on an unwise acquisition.

CONCLUSION

I very much hope you've enjoyed this second book of mine and that it will inspire you to get involved in more sophisticated and bigger deals.

Usually, the bigger the deal, the bigger the risk and the larger the loss that you could potentially make. This puts many people off doing deals larger than those of a size they are comfortable with. However, hopefully the information I have shared here will encourage you to look at greater and more profitable opportunities, and that you will have learned how you can minimise the risks involved.

As I am sure you are now aware, it can be an exciting lifestyle, and with it comes enormous pride and satisfaction that you have created or transformed some part of this country's property heritage – a great achievement

After all, where would this country be without developers and investors, who have the drive, vision and ambition to transform, update and increase the residential housing stock – along with commercial developments – and who have improved the population's quality of life in this country today?

Also available from Matador books:

John Howard's Inside Guide to
Property Development & Investment for Newcomers